SHOUT IT OUT

Healing Your Wounds With God's Amazing Love

LINDA BERRY

Linda Berry

Jeremiah 29:11

xulon PRESS

ISBN 9781498468084

www.xulonpress.com

ENDORSEMENTS

first met Linda on a trip to Kansas City to attend the World Revival Church. She was my husband's boss. Linda had expressed a desire to have a travel companion on the trip and my husband had suggested me. "You will be great together!" he had said.

Setting out on an eight hour drive to spend a long week-end with someone I had never met really was out of character for me, but God must have been in it. I agreed to go as long as we could spend some time at the international House of Prayer while we were there.

We "hit it off" immediately and returned from the trip like old friends. What made us such a perfect match?

We both had a hunger to seek more of God. We wanted to experience Him in His fullness. We both knew that healing, help, and wholeness rested in His character and presence; and nothing was more satisfying than an encounter with the living God.

Since that time, as I have gotten to know more of Linda's story, I have been amazed and touched by her willingness to not only open herself up to the loving Heavenly surgeon, but to share that experience with others. Her desire is that they too might come to a place of restoration and joy as they experience Him as Jehovah Raphe, the God who heals.

Linda and I continue to share the desire to see God bind up the broken-hearted, and I am pleased to have a small part as she releases her story, which I am certain will touch hearts, and change lives into eternity.

Linda O'Toole - *Program Director of Set-Free Reading*

The first book Linda wrote (Broken Chains) was just the beginning of what God has done in her life. Since then Linda has realized that forgiveness is more than words being spoken. Forgiveness is allowing God to change you from your head to your heart. God has anointed Linda to minister to other hurting people, and I believe that this book will be a blessing to others walking through any type of abuse.

Shirley Thomas - *Friend from Friendship Baptist Church*

The first time Linda and I met, Linda shared her story of how she overcame one tragedy after another. Though the pain, shame, and embarrassment had haunted her for decades she was finally free. Linda shared secrets not only of how she was put into bondage, but how God's miraculous and divine appointments can set us free. Get ready for an unforgettable ride to freedom as you read Linda's true story!

Sherry "Sourer" Pittman - *TV Host of "Survive and Thrive," Heart to Heart, and inspirational writer.*

I met Linda in late 2009. Her heart's desire was to have a more intimate walk with the Lord but there were situations in her life that needed to be healed. I agreed to help her to walk through the issues controlling her life that she might become victorious over the past. Linda had to reach the point of knowing that she was valuable, loved, and worthy of being set free from her past to move forward; and that meant becoming vulnerable and speaking the truth into her life. I believe that this book will help others who have been abused not to wait until they are in the later years of life to deal with the issues caused by abuse.

Alice Burnes - Test reader and friend, former employee of Rape Information Counseling Service.

I've known Linda for over twenty years. Besides becoming close friends, we attended the same church. About five years ago, Linda wanted a closer walk with God. God sent people into her life to help her deal with the abuse of her past. She has leaned on the Great Physician for her healing.

Elaine Munos - *Business owner of a child care facility.*

ACKNOWLEDGEMENTS

Without God I am nothing. I am loved, blessed, and set free because of His extravagant love for me. He loved me when I was broken, healed me when I didn't think it was possible, and set me free to worship Him.

IT IS TIME TO SHOUT IT OUT!

I am thankful for the morning devotional and prayer group who have always encouraged me to grow in the Lord and taught me how to discuss issues, be open and vulnerable. Their words of wisdom, prayers, and encouragement have given me the strength to press on. I am blessed by the stories of victory over abuse that have been shared with me, and pray for victory for every woman, child, or man who needs to know they are loved by God unconditionally.

I am indebted to my dear friend and sister in the Lord, Alice Burnes who always speaks the truth into my life, encourages me to grow, loves me unconditionally, and confronts the issues that have had power over my life. Her compassionate heart, Godly love, and life have displayed God's love and given me strength when I wanted to quit. Her willingness to take on the responsibility of teaching me accountability and helping me walk through the effects of sexual abuse has strengthened my walk with the Lord.

I thank God for the support from my friends at South Seventh Assembly of God and Friendship Baptist Church. Their prayers and encouragement have sustained me when I have faltered and carried me when I was weak.

INTRODUCTION

Look and watch, and be utterly amazed. For I am going to do something
In your days that you would not believe, even if you were told.

Habakkuk 1:5

Do I believe that I am special and loved?

I challenge you to walk through the darkness with me, remove the scars, take off
the masks you have been hiding behind and receive the complete healing that only
God can do. The road is not easy and can only be completed by total honesty and surrendering all of your life to Jesus. Today in our prayer group a statement was made
that touched my heart and made me cry out to God. I must feel the pain before I can
make the change. Do I want to do that? Not really! We can no longer lie to ourselves.
Healing comes from what you say about yourself. I am special, loved, and have value,
but the question is do I believe that I am loved and have value?

Will I ever be whole? I can if I take back the power from my abusers. Sexual
abuse is not about love, it is about sexual gratification for the abuser. There is no quick
answer for healing of the abuse. Confronting the abuser, the issues, and getting into
counseling is a step towards healing but will not heal the inner child that has been so
deeply wounded. God is the only one who can cleanse every wound, take the shame
away, and heal us internally. But do we really believe that God will do it for us?

We must find the courage to speak the truth, and let go of what we can't change.
We need to shout it out! Silence is not always golden! I cannot do it for you. Do I
sometimes walk in fear or disobedience, yes! Do I sometimes take the masks off and
put them back on the same day, yes! Do I want to visit the pain to be healed? Probably
not! But without being honest and facing the pain there is no victory. Even as I have
asked myself, I ask you today, what event or person affected your view of what love
is about. Do you feel really loved or just used? My father said he loved me at the
age of five, but love is not about molesting a child or promising that child gifts if she
doesn't tell anyone. If that is love, I want no part of it, then or now!

Many of us have suffered internal "burns" that have ravaged our emotions and scarred our hearts. For a burn to heal, we must rid ourselves of the old skin, cleansing the wound again and again in order to promote healing. Burns must be excised or cut away within the first week. It is an excruciating painful process to go through. You may have been sexually molested only once but your inner child has suffered a blow that is difficult to heal. Most survivors of sexual abuse have been abused for many years and have been explicitly told to never tell anyone.

My desire in writing this book is that I, too, will be completely healed. You see, there are days I want to stay hidden. I begin to question God, can you see me sitting in the darkness? Do you really love me enough to save me from myself? I have tried so hard not to cry, not to feel the pain of rejection, and not to care if I am loved. I have tried to pretend I am not angry, not to run away, and not to attempt to take my life. But for so long I felt like a sexual object, just a child playing at being an adult. I didn't want to be the mommy or wife; I wanted to be that little girl who used to run, jump, laugh, and play.

Sexual abuse is not about love, no matter how many times your abuser tells you that they love you. Let's be honest, it is not about loving you, it is gratification for the abuser. After a period of time you may feel pleasure because God made our bodies sexual. During those times I was angry, felt dirty, and just wanted to die.

I, too need to take off the masks, tear off the scars, and apply the healing balm of God's love and the sacrifice of the death of Christ to my wounds. His love walks through the tears, sees your pain, and turns the darkness into light. While walking the pathway to recovery one set of footprints may be all you see. Not once does God say figure it out on your own. Instead He clearly says, Trust me. Trust me when you can't see the end of the journey. I will be the one walking beside you.

God's message to us is always unconditional love. I've never quit loving you and never will. Expect love, love, and more love. My love will never leave you alone. Because one woman chose to confront the issue of abuse in my life with unconditional love, God has brought me through many of the issues of abuse. Love walks through the pain and brings healing. I am loved even though I have been broken and shattered into many pieces. The pain never completely heals, it seems to pop back up every once in a while, but we serve a God who loves healing and wholeness. While we may never be as good as new, we can receive emotional healing here on earth.

Brian Welch says and I quote:

"Until you heal the wounds of your past, you are going to bleed. You can bandage the bleeding with food, with alcohol, with drugs, with work, with cigarettes, and with sex. But eventually. It will all ooze through and stain your life. You must find the strength to open the wounds, stick your hands inside, pull out the core of the pain that is holding you in your past, and the memories and make peace with them."

Shout it out! God heals and restores broken lives. He delivers and sets free all who are in bondage. The chains can be broken!

CONTENTS

THE VALLEY OF THE SHADOW OF DEATH

October, 1985

Psalms: 23:4-5
Even though I walk through the valley of the shadow of death, I will fear no evil, for you are with me, your rod and your staff, they comfort me.

Although the beginning of this story is not in chronological order, it is at this time, September 1985, I began to realize the depth of my depression and that I needed to reach out for help. My husband died suddenly while we were traveling and I was overwhelmed with the loss and decisions that had to be made. I had no hope and didn't know who to turn to. It was at this time I began writing my story, a story that spoke of deep depression and desperation. My life seemed to have no value. On September 5th, I lost the two people I knew that loved me, my husband and my aunt. I was devastated, suicidal, and unable to cope although I would have never admitted it.

I sat in the motel room for over three hours while the coroner came, and the police searched the whole room. I was questioned again and again about the blood in the bathroom. Because my husband's death was in a town away from home I had to answer questions for over three hours while his body was lying at my feet. They were insistent upon doing an autopsy but I would not let them do it because my husband wanted to give his body to help others. The officers would not let me call anyone until they were finished questioning me. I was distraught, crying, and screaming. I needed to talk to someone, but I was denied.

Finally they made a call to Geraldine, my friend and allowed her to talk with me. She insisted that they allow me to at least take my blood pressure medicine. I wanted to talk to my Aunt Hannah but after the officers had talked to my uncle they told me my aunt had been in a serious accident and was probably not going to make it. My aunt on that same day four hours earlier asked me when I was going to give my heart to the Lord. I didn't believe that God really loved me, and the pain was too great to share; so I flippantly answered her that I didn't know. Even at this time I still didn't believe that God could love me, a woman so abused and broken.

As my husband and I were traveling back home that same day from a two-week vacation, we were talking about our marriage and some things we needed to do. My husband said to me that day the only thing he regretted about our marriage was that I wasn't a Christian. Four hours later my husband died suddenly in our hotel room. My heart was overwhelmed with anger at God. I cried out "Why, God, why?" When is enough trauma in my life enough? God was silent once again. Or was I even listening? Could I hear him speaking to me amidst the pain? Where is God when my heart is broken and I need him?

Although, I do not remember being suicidal someone from mental health arrived and refused to allow me to take any of my medications until they had talked with Geraldine. Shortly after that they allowed me to make a call to a friend from Springfield to come and be with me. I was in the room where my husband laid dead at my feet until my friends from Springfield came to be with me.

When my friends arrived that evening at the motel, the person from the mental health department said I had to go to the hospital to be checked out. I refused to stay at the hospital, I just wanted to go home but by this time it was 2:00 A.M. We went back to the motel and got another room. I sat on the bathroom floor crying all night.

Driving home the next day was a nightmare. At times I was driving twenty five miles an hour on the highway, other times way over the speed limit. My friend finally stopped and said she wanted her son to ride with me because she knew I loved him and would not drive so erratically. I loved her dearly but thought she had lost her mind when she said she wanted Chad to ride with me. Chad was crying because he loved my husband who was his only father figure.

We finally arrived in Springfield and went to the funeral home only to find out that my husband's body had been taken directly to the hospital. For the next few weeks, I walked through the narrow, winding, seemingly never ending valley of the shadow of death. Around each crevice, there seemed to be only a bottomless pit of frozen, and barren ground. Death like the sting of frostbite, and unrelieved pain, separated me from the love of my life.

One of the last things my husband said to me was that he wished I knew his Jesus. I felt like I had betrayed my husband by never accepting Christ as my Lord. Many times I kept him at home on Sundays by turning the alarm off. I wanted to believe but just couldn't understand why God didn't intervene during all the years of abuse.

The time came when I had to go home where my father was residing. My husband and I had taken him in and had not found a place for him to live before we went on vacation. I was overwhelmed and scared that he would try to abuse me again. But I was in no condition to deal with him. I only wanted him to be somewhere else, and to be gone quickly.

I remember little about the memorial service for my husband, in September. The doctor had given me tranquilizers for the first two weeks after the death of my husband. I was numb and yet a little crazy as I tried to deal with all the things that needed to be done. My friend Peggy found a bottle of tranquilizers on my dresser and asked why any doctor would give a person a prescription where you took one pill for every 10 pounds. We cried and laughed over the prescription until I realized it was for my dog when we took him in the car with us. Then we just set on the floor and cried together. Shortly after that as we were cleaning out the closet I found all the liquor that had been stuck in the back of the closet from the previous years' Christmas party at work. As we poured it down the kitchen sink, we sang how dry I am! There were a lot of times of tears, a few of laughter, and just a lot of pain as we worked together.

My husband was supposed to be transferred to a funeral home in Springfield but because he had stipulated on his driver's license he wanted to donate his body to science, I never had the opportunity to see him again. It was five months later before I had any closure. I received his remains back, had a memorial service for him on Valentine's Day with my counselor Sister Margaret Dolan officiating. As a part of the grief recovery she had me plan and write the service.

My relationship with my mother escalated during this time. She refused to come to the funeral although she had plenty of offers from my family and friends to bring her. I didn't want her to come because of me but because of all the things my husband had done for her. Staying at home with her cat was more important than being with her daughter during this time of sorrow. I was enraged at her callous attitude and never wanted to see her again.

Shattered and broken in spirit I contemplated my own death, as I angrily lashed out to God. Why God? Is there no end to this overwhelming sorrow and pain I must bear? Is there any reason for living? Is death an escape? I simply cannot deal with going back to my home. How will I be able to deal with my abusive father without my husband there to intervene? Do you really love me God? God was silent. I really don't know why I expected him to answer me.

My soul knew that death was just the beginning of intolerable anguish, a fire unquenchable; for neither did I know or serve the God of my deceased husband. Yet in this valley with its high and lofty mountains, I still cried out. Where is this God my husband loved? My heart is broken and crushed beneath this heavy load, darkness descends upon me and I am so afraid. Unbidden tears pour down my cheeks as I cry out in anguish. It seems that the light at the end of the valley is dim, flickering, and now gone. A deep darkness surrounds me. The depression was like a heavy blanket that was wrapped about me and it was too heavy for me to remove.

The situation continued to escalate as my father became more aggressive and abusive to anyone who came into my home. He accused me of sleeping with a black pastor who came to my home to buy my husband's fishing and hunting equipment for his youth group. Incidents of sexual insinuations became common each night I came home to fix his meals. The state laws said since he was a senior I could not move him out without his consent.

One night I came home and found him waiting for me completely naked in the living room. He told me what he was going to do to me in language I cannot repeat. I screamed out in rage, literally threw him in his room and said I would kill him with my husband's gun if he came out of the room. At that moment I hated him and wanted him to die a slow agonizing death. I called my friend crying and screaming, and she came over immediately to my home. I was beyond dealing with my father and afraid that I would kill him. I went to stay with Susan and her son Chad. We contacted my doctor who agreed to help me find a place for him. All I had to do was get him in to see the doctor. One week later my friend Susan and I took him to a boarding home until we could find a better place for him. I had only minimal contact with my father during the next year, but I still had to oversee his care as I was his legal guardian.

Psalms 116:3 speaks of what my heart was feeling. "The cords of death entangled me, the anguish of the grave came upon me; I was overcome by trouble and sorrow."

Fear and despair tormented me. I functioned each day as I went to work but the nights I spend crying and taking tranquillizers. Fierce storms assailed my soul. My mind cowers in billows of doubt. My spirit falters, stumbles, and cries out. My God, my God, have you totally forsaken me? Darkness and despair surround me, each step I take becomes more difficult, and I don't think I can survive one more day, or even one more hour, or one more heartache. Like a ship, my body and soul are tossed unmercifully on the rocks in the stormy sea. I feel like I am crushed into a thousand pieces, as I fall into the depths of the sea.

Heartbroken, I crash upon the boulders, flaying against the mighty waves, struggling to reach the lifeline that was thrown to me. Despair overwhelms me as I realize I am rushing down into the pit of hell. Desperately I scream, Jesus are you real?

Then I hear a sweet voice saying, "He that believes in me shall never die. Come my child. Let us walk together." Reaching out, I gripped His hand. Then I saw the green pastures, a place of rest for my weary soul. Exhausted I lay down in the green pastures, protected by the Good Shepherd. When I woke up, He led me beside the still waters. My broken dreams I laid at His feet. I felt no fear as long as He was walking with me. His rod and staff brought me comfort.

At this time, my love starved heart realized His love had no limit. But the barriers I had set up stopped me from believing that He loved me. Thanksgiving week came. We had been married ten years on the day before Thanksgiving. I took the week off from work and begin to take Xanax every time I woke up. My friend Freda called and realized I was totally drugged. She told me to open the house door so she could get in. She came over and said she was taking me to the hospital but I refused to go. She then made a pot of strong coffee and made me drink coffee and walk until I was exhausted and went back to sleep. I had never drank coffee! Nor do I want to ever drink it again!

Christmas is just around the corner. I want to make this Christmas special for the three children my husband and I had volunteered to help through the Big Brother and Sister program. I knew this would be the last Christmas we would share. Amanda, Missy, and Chad were heartbroken at the loss of my husband.

It's the night before Christmas, the night we always spent with the children, the night we sang Christmas carols, played in the snow, danced around the room, waiting until that perfect time to open the presents. This Christmas is so different. The children just want to talk about Bob. We sat around the tree talking about all the things the kids remembered about Bob. We sang Christmas songs and recorded them so they could remember this Christmas.

Earlier that day Chad and I picked up the hamster for Amanda. My husband had already got the hamster cage, toys and food for the hamster. Amanda cried when she opened her presents for she knew the gift was from Bob. She asked me if she could name the hamster BJB after my husband.

Chad misses Bob so much. He just sits and pets his dog. Then he begins to cry. My heart is broken as all the kids began to cry. Chad asked if he could have Bob's dog for Christmas. I hug him and we cry together as he remembers all the fun he had with my husband and the dog. We called his mother and she agreed to let Chad have the dog.

Missy, the youngest of the three children we had is quiet as she cuddles in my arms. She wants to know why she can't go and see my husband. She remembers the time Santa Claus came to her house and wants to know if it was my husband.

The next few months I was in counseling but unable to talk about the sexual or physical abuse. I could barely talk about the death of my husband. I did not cry while I was with my counselor. I could not seem to move on. The pain was overwhelming, and as always I stuffed all my feelings when I was around people.

Drugs became my way of existing. I was able to work but still not dealing with the sorrow. My physician refused to give me any more medication instead insisted that I see a psychiatrist. After being in the doctor's office for over two hours with the psychiatrist, they had no evidence that could keep me in the hospital. The next day I made an appointment with another doctor who prescribed Xanax for me and continued to do so for over twenty years.

Throughout the next few months I attempted to take my life by using drugs excessively in the evening. Again and again God intervened. It was as if God was using everyone in my life to tell me that He cared for me. Many of my friends that were Christians were praying for me and constantly checking on me.

The night came when I planned to go back to where my husband died. I requested the same room, and had enough drugs to end my life. I made the plans and left my friend a letter in her mailbox. God intervened that night. My friend never collected her mail usually until Saturday but she found the letter that night, and told my counselor what I was doing. Sister Margaret begin calling me. Finally I answered my phone. She talked me into coming back and meeting with her. She could've had me put into the hospital but instead she stayed with me and prayed for me. That night I spent in the garden of God ministered to by one of His angels.

The Garden of God

One day in our bereavement
Awakening we begin to see
A new life we must begin
Feelings of hope breaking open
The dry earth beneath our grief.

Tiny little sprouts of joy
Breaking through the hard ground
Harden by our constant weeping
Surely, a garden wants to grow
In the desert of our sorrow.

Make us new, O' Lord
Bring us into newness of life
Let us see the desert of our sorrow,
Blooming with flowers of joy
Peace, and love once again.

New life where there was no life
Seeds sprouting into being
Like the dawn of a new day,
Springing forth with beautiful
Brightly colored plants of joy.

A garden of the fruit of the Spirit
Nurtured by God, the Master planter,

Growing in the desert of our life
Bringing forth comfort and healing
To all who pass thru this pathway.

It was time to heal from the grief and move on. A poem written by Martha Nicholson seems to help me as I accept that I must move forward.

TEACH ME TO WALK ALONE

I live now in a strange new land
Where I must walk alone
Where I must smile without a tear
And grief must make no moan.
My comfort and my guiding star
My tower of strength has gone
No peace ascends to me with dusk,
No light breaks with my dawn.
The habit of his loving heart,
Was thoughtfulness for me?
And yet that heart has ceased to beat,
Lord, how can such things be?
My arms have found if they reach out
They clasp but empty air
And though I search the silent rooms
I never find him there.
I had to learn to walk, dear Lord,
When I was young and small
Teach me again for of myself
I can do naught at all.

Thus began a journey seeking healing and restoration for my broken life. Nine months later, I surrendered my life to Jesus. It was just the beginning of the path of restoration that God wanted to complete in my life. I was still walking in denial and secrecy concerning the sexual abuse, unable to claim the victory that God wanted in my life. What had been sown in tears and heartbreak God wanted to heal but I wasn't ready to reveal to anyone the abuse I had been subjected to.

My counselor realized the issues I was dealing with were more than just the grief of losing my husband. She arranged and paid for me to attend a conference on sexual abuse even though I had never told her I was abused. I agreed to attend but was totally overwhelmed with what I was seeing and experiencing at this conference. Hundreds of people were there, many of them having been in counseling for years. Many were carrying around dolls or other objects that represented their inner child. From each class I attended I heard the words when you finish this conference you will not believe there is a god that cares about you.

I had only been a Christian for about three weeks, and my heart was deeply troubled. I attended all the classes but received nothing that benefited me in dealing with the sexual abuse. The last class was on anger where the instructor locked the door and provided different ways for us to express our anger. I was terrified with what I was hearing and just wanted to leave. The instructor told me I needed to stay and express my anger at those who had abused me. My anger that day was totally directed at the instructor. I told him he would open the door and let me out or I would report him to the police. I had my cell phone in my hand ready to call the police so he said okay, I will let you leave but you are making a mistake in leaving. I ran out of the conference center and went to church. With tears streaming down from my eyes I walked into the church. The congregation surrounded me with prayer and love without even knowing why I was so distraught.

God sent forth His love to minister to me once again. I was broken but still He loved me. Nothing is too difficult for Him. As we start this journey of faith, healing and deliverance, I do not promise you the road will be easy. But this I am confident of, through the flood and the flame, through the fire of brokenness, God has never forsaken me. He passionately pursues my heart, seeking to heal every broken part.

My desire is to be a vessel that my Master, Jesus can use for His glory. He's mending and cleansing this vessel of clay. He's speaking to my heart, there is a work you must do. I have prepared you to minister to other broken innocent women and children. As you pour out to others, I will pour into you my love and strength.

Walk with me through this journey as we both seek complete healing and restoration in our lives. I am broken but still loved. Today, I can choose to be wherever my life experience takes me, and I am free to be the woman God created. I can choose my behavior, be in charge of my own self-worth, and learn to love myself and others.

CLIMBING UPWARD

The mountains in their majestic splendor
Impart strength to my fainting heart
As onward I trudge, clinging to the thought
That tomorrow I may scale the heights
To stretch and reach to the uttermost limits
Allowing my spirit to soar and fly free.

The road narrow, and seemingly never ending
Leads me through the valleys, over the rocks
Winding its way to the pinnacle of the mountain
Rocks along the pathway cause me to stumble
Boulders cause me to retreat, seeking a different way

But I must continue to seek the highest peak
Onward I must go, seeking the right pathway
Pressing on until the prize I'm striving for, I gain.
By faith I will reach the pinnacle and hear Jesus say
Well done, my faithful daughter, come on home.

Then I will walk through the pearly gates
Down the streets of gold where Jesus reigns
There will be no death, no sickness, and no tears
I will then sing that song "Amazing Grace"
And look upon my redeemer's face for eternity.

CREATED IN GOD'S IMAGE

It is July, 1946

A little squiggly sperm joined an egg in my mother's womb, just a little dot that would someday grow into a child. My frame was not hidden from God when I was made in the secret place. He saw me there and loved every molecule of my development. He created me exactly the way He wanted me to be. He knew whether I would have the X or Y chromosome, be a girl or a boy.

God kept me in that warm cocoon sheltering me with His love. He is an amazing God because in the thousands of years no one even has the same finger-prints as I do. He knew the time I was conceived, the time I would be born. He set the date. On April 25th, 1947, my mother brought me into this world. I wonder if she really wanted a little girl. But at least she didn't abort me.

God had his hand upon my life from the day forward or did He? I was fear-fully and wonderfully made complete with all ten fingers and toes, and had the ability to grow and think. I often wondered if I was an accident. Did my parents want another child or did they just not know about birth control? It doesn't really matter anymore because now I know God had a plan for me.

God knew the pain and the abuse I would walk through, but it was not His choice nor in His plan for my life. Did I always believe that God loved me? No, I didn't. Many times I was angry at God and wished I had not been born. I fought the anger and resentment that rose to the surface, unwanted and uninvited. What happened to my mommy that caused her to cast me aside as if I was an old rag doll not worthy of her love and attention?

I have often asked God, "Why me?" I wore the mask of "Why me" for many years as I watched other children with loving parents, mommies and daddies that hugged and kissed their children. Why God, did you give me parents that would beat me, slap me, burn me, and sexually abuse me? Was it because I didn't think you were a good father as my first Sunday school teacher told me? I cried out in anger to a God I could not understand. My heart cried out what is the value of a life that is destroyed by abusive parents?

But God gave his creation a choice to serve Him or to disobey. No matter what the circumstances, always remind yourself that God's love for you gives you courage to carry on and to be real. It is that love and His presence with us that is enough to carry us through the storms of our lives. We know that when He is with us, the storm can't sink us. "The Lord watches over all who love him." Psalms 145:20

"When our world begins to crumble, we may forget that our value is not found in our doing, but in who we are." (Cara Joynet)

One day in April, 1949, I must have been a very bad little girl. My mommy was angry, picked me up and attempted to kill me by pouring hot water over me. But God stepped into the room when my aunt heard me screaming and it was only my leg that was burned. I still carry that scar on my leg where my mother poured hot water on me. Because of this I didn't walk until I was over two years old. When I was old enough I asked my mother what had happened to my leg. She said that I was a bad little girl who was playing in the tub and turned on the hot water. I wondered how I got into the tub when I couldn't walk. I questioned my aunt about the incident when I was older and she told me my mommy was just holding me and spilled hot water on me. When I was a teenager my aunt told me the whole story- that my mom didn't want a baby girl. That scar became a token of great shame as children mocked me. One day a doctor asked me how I got the scar. I wanted to hide and lie but that day I spoke the truth. The doctor wept and said, "I am so sorry."

It is just a physical scar of abuse but how many of us carry around each day the burdens of emotional scars that we are afraid to share with anyone. The emotional scars that I carried for over fifty years are so much greater than the physical scars which healed within a short time.

Approximately three years later in April, 1952, a day I will never forget; my father sexually abused me under the disguise that he loved me. That day I lost the innocence of a child and became afraid of my daddy and the dark. Up to this time I had always been daddy's little girl. I would run to him with my big dolly running beside me as I dragged her along. It was a beautiful spring day in Iowa. We lived on a farm with lots of animals and I loved to go outside to play; but on this particular day my aunt and my mother took my two brothers and sister with them to go someplace for the day. I was left at home with my father and uncle, my dad's twin brother.

For a while I played with my big doll that my daddy had given me when I was three years old. I was cooking dinner in my little make- believe kitchen while daddy and my uncle were drinking beer in the dining room. Daddy said I couldn't go outside because I might get lost or hurt.

Soon daddy called me into the dining room and said he had a couple of presents for me. It was close to my fifth birthday and I wanted two dresses for school, a red one and a red plaid dress. Red was my favorite color. Daddy gave me those two dresses and told me to take off all my clothes and try them on. He sat me on his lap and then he touched me in my private parts, and made me touch him. I got all sticky, so he ran the water and gave me a bath still touching me, and telling me I was a good little girl and someday I would have breasts like my mommy. Then he told me that I could never tell anyone what happened. It was our secret and I was so special. I begin crying and couldn't stop crying and asked daddy why he had hurt me. I hated that I had no control over when and how these episodes of crying would occur. Sometimes they just appeared when my daddy walked into the room, or when my mother shouted at me.

I was told to go to bed and stay there because I had been bad. Daddy said I would get into a lot of trouble if I ever told anyone. I cried myself to sleep and threw my big doll on the floor. I didn't want to be with my daddy anymore. I just wanted to run away and hide, but there was no place to go. I often went to the barn and climbed up into the hay loft where I could play with the kittens. Sometimes I would sneak off and go down to the road where a sweet little old lady would read to me. She made the best sugar cookies. She always told me I was a good little girl and I could visit her anytime.

I became a very introverted sad little girl who didn't want anyone to touch her. I didn't run and laugh anymore. I was very careful not to let my guard down. One Sunday I got up really early. I got some cereal to eat and ran all the way down to the church on the corner. I wanted to meet this Jesus my aunt talked about. She said He loved little children like me. At church that day I heard that God was like our daddies. He loved little children and would protect us. Our Sunday school picture was of children surrounding Jesus and sitting on His lap. I never wanted to sit on my daddy's lap after that day in April, 1952. Where was Jesus in the years that followed as I was continually sexually molested? There was no safe place to hide. My parents always found me and punished me for hiding.

The abuse continued and became more and more violent as I grew up. I had no one I could tell. But one day I decided to tell my mother. She was letting me help her in the kitchen making cookies. My mother became very angry, slapped me and told me to quit lying to her. Then she told me if I was telling the truth it was better that it was happening to me than her. She said I had better not tell anyone or she would beat me until I couldn't talk. She didn't care nor did she intervene. It seemed like she just became more abusive after I told her what was happening. I think that was the day I begin to hate my mother. Where could a little girl run to? There was nowhere to hide and no one to protect me.

Today I know God expresses His love and protection for His people, but He doesn't stop others from making the wrong decisions. We are not robots programmed to act in a certain way. How many times have we come close to death and not even realized it? God has created and redeemed us; we belong to him and He knows each one of us by name. His word states that He is the perfect protector. He delivers us and saves us from our enemies. But where was God the day my daddy hurt me? Where was God when my mother slapped me and called me a liar? Did He care that I cried for hours? His word says He will protect us from trouble and surround us with songs of deliverance. Where was God that day? Why didn't He deliver me from the abuse?

Years went by and I could see no way of deliverance from the constant abuse. So you ask, even as I have asked, why did God allow this? Did He not see the abuse? Did He not care that my parents were physically and sexually abusing me? Did He not see the fear I faced each time my father came home drunk? Did He just stand by when my mother burned me, beat me and called me a whore? I didn't even know what being a whore was. I asked my aunt and she wanted to know where I heard that word.

There was never a safe place to hide and I didn't believe there was a God that cared. The scars were placed upon my body and Jesus wept. He bore my shame and scars at the cross. He was beaten, forced to carry the cross that He would be nailed to. His side was pierced, and a crown of thorns placed upon His head. He died for you and me. Every praise belongs to Him for He has brought me through years of sexual abuse and rape. I am still here, broken but still loved. I find it difficult to accept that God loves me. I feel like a broken flower pot that is never quite put back together- it still is cracked and seems to be of no use.

God wants to repair the broken vessels. He will give us a life of joy and peace. He will replace the violence with healing, and give you victory. He will replace isolation with His presence, rejection with acceptance and low self-esteem by giving you the power to become an overcomer. The power of evil around you is no match for the power of God's love in you and for you. You can daily exercise your authority over the enemy. God hears your prayers, knows your struggles, and wants you to call on His name. He came that we might be made whole though Him.

Is the road to victory easy, no way! I often have nightmares that wake me up screaming. Each time I hear of innocent children being sexually abused or even raped my heart breaks. I was one of those children that was molested. I was told never to tell. Daddy said he loved me. I was just an object for his pleasure. To me love hurts and has caused me to not be able to accept love from others and even at times doubt that God loves me. How do you love someone when you get no love in return? How do you love without being trapped or used by the other person? You say you love me but I don't believe you. My answer always to people who told me they loved me was yeah, sure. What do you want from me? I didn't believe that anyone loved me for just me. But God did! I will shout it out that God loves me. He is able to deliver and set us free!

I thought I had to somehow earn God's love. But He was only waiting for me to accept what He had already done. When we accept His unconditional love, it changes us from the inside out. Jesus came to heal our broken hearts. We cannot do it alone. Even as I write this book it is difficult for me to accept that others love me, and that God loves me just as I am, broken and unable to put the pieces of my life back together without His help.

He took me from my brokenness into a realm of love. He bound up my love-starved heart and replaced it with a new heart filled with His love. Through the process I learned I didn't have to earn God's love. I came to Him with all my baggage, fears, and regrets, and He replaced them with His forgiveness and boundless love. He didn't care if I came to him angry or so depressed that I couldn't believe anyone really loved me; He simply loved his broken daughter.

Jesus came to set the prisoners free, and to heal the brokenhearted. Do you think that quite possibly the crowd was shocked by the words of Jesus? They expected a mighty warrior, a King, not someone who would set the captives free. They didn't expect a heart surgeon but He came that we might be made whole.

I came to Christ broken, expecting Jesus to make me whole, but still trying to do it in my own strength and knowledge. The power of the cross does not come through what we do, but through what Jesus has already done. My hurting heart sent me running down pathways that I now regret. I was searching for love and deliverance in all the wrong places.

Jesus knew the day that my father abused me, a child of just five years old. I didn't understand the pain that my father inflicted on me and then told me that he loved me. He said it was our secret but if this was love I wanted nothing to do with it. God's heart cried out but He had given every man and woman the choice to serve Him.

As a child I was sexually abused for many years by more than one man and by two of my brothers. The pain and suffering caused deep rooted feelings of isolation, rejection, anger, guilt, and low self-esteem. I didn't know what true love was or how to be emotionally healed. I withdrew into a world of books and silence.

The wound of a child feeling unwanted, rejected, and sexually abused is a wound that goes so deep into the heart of the child that the child ends up being an adult that feels worthless and doesn't have the ability to love. Sexual abuse is an invasion of a child's heart and soul and most often comes from someone who should be protecting the child. The after effect is that the child does not know who to trust or to reach out to for love and protection. I was that child, unable to love or trust anyone. I had a bad attitude when anyone came close to me. I often put my hands up, backed off and said don't touch me.

Still God loved me, and promised to heal every hurt that I had ever endured. Whatever period of life you are in, Jesus is always waiting for you to call out His name. He is Alpha and Omega, the beginning and the end and everything in between.

He said, I've come to open the eyes of the blind. I've come to set the prisoner free. I've come to heal the brokenhearted. Are you seeking healing, love, or restoration? For years I wanted someone just to love me but all I knew was that love hurt.

WHAT GOD DID FOR ME, HE WILL DO FOR YOU!

God wants to restore your life, give you joy and peace. In the place of our greatest shame and self-condemnation, our most significant act of spiritual warfare is choosing to believe God still loves us. Try as I might, I cannot quite grasp how deep and perfect God's love is for me.

I SIMPLY CANNOT WRAP MY MIND AROUND THAT KIND OF LOVE.

He lives in me, knows everything about me, including my deepest desires and darkest secrets and yet He still loves me. He understands all the things that happened in my life including the things which are still to come. His love is boundless and everlasting.

A friend gave me a big reindeer with the words Jesus Loves Me on one of its feet. Each time I gaze upon that reindeer sitting on my bookcase in my computer room, I speak the words out into the atmosphere to remind myself that Jesus loves me. Yes, he loves me.

I urge you to open your heart to receive vast amounts of His love. The more of His love that is in your heart, the less room there is for fear. Perfect love (God's love) casts out all fear. The cross of Jesus is where our greatest fears were conquered once and for all. God cares about you, knows all your struggles, and wants you to call upon Him.

He shelters you in His arms, comforts you when the road seems too long, the valley too deep to climb out, the mountains too high to climb up. You may never understand why everything has happened in your life nor why it is difficult for you to trust, or to reach out to others and allow them to input love into your life; but you can trust the love of God. For years, I trusted God only with the things I thought he could handle. Or was it that I wanted to be in control? I couldn't release the pain to God, still God saw the broken child I was and loved me.

Jeremiah 17:7-8

Blessed is the man who trusts in the Lord, whose trust is the Lord. He is like a tree planted by water, that sends its roots by the stream, and does not fear when heat comes, for its leaves remain green, and is not anxious in the year of draught, for it does not cease to bear fruit.

Just take a moment to answer these questions before moving on.
1. What gives value to your life?
2. Whom do you trust and why?
3. Do you feel worthy of being loved?
4. Or do you feel that you must perform perfectly and avoid all mistakes to be loved?
5. Did you ever tell anyone what was happening when you were abused!

JUST FOR YOU

I hear your voice saying, I did it just for you.
I bore your pain, that you might be healed
I wore the crown of thorns just for you
The nails pierced my hands and feet
Just for you I suffered, my child.
That's how much I love you.

I cried out to my Father, if it be possible
Let this cup pass from me, however
My Father not as I will, but as you will
I thirsted but did not yield to temptation
Or drink of the bitter gall to dull the pain
Just for you I suffered, my child.
That's how much I love you.

The pain, the shame, I carried to the cross
None watched and prayed while I agonized
Still I cried out to my father, thy will be done
I willingly gave my life just for you.
Two men hung beside me, one went to paradise
Crying out in a loud voice, forgive me.
I did it for him and just for you.
That's how much I loved the world.

The other mocked me and died alone
Suffering the death of the cross
No hope, no chance for forgiveness
You see, the cost he didn't count.
I held nothing back- just paid the price
That you might have eternal life.
That's how much I love you.

HIDING BEHIND MASKS

C ome, walk with me. It is the time of the year when the seasons are changing, things are dying, and God is preparing us for a winter season. It is as if all of God's various trees, and beautiful flowers have put on colorful masks, camouflaging what they were meant to be. Soon all the beautiful leaves will fall, the flowers will die and the trees will be stripped of their glory to a bare and bleak existence until spring. It appears that the trees put on a stark mask of depression until spring comes when once again they become fruitful. How I wish I could put on a disguise so that my daddy and mommy couldn't recognize me and I could find a safe place to hide.

Halloween is just around the corner; children are preparing their costumes and masks to go trick and treating. It is one day out of a year, but how many of us wear our masks year round, hoping no one will see the real person hidden behind that happy face? A smile is just a mask you wear if you want to hide your pain. Hiding behind masks are untold stories, secrets that have been hidden for years, and I was living in a shell hiding whom I was meant to be. There is a face behind the mask, but is it me? I have worn many masks throughout my life, none of them having anything to do with Halloween. If I took a mask off I replaced it with another one, depending on where I was going and what I was going to be doing.

Hiding behind a mask labeled performance was my favorite mask. I thought if I did enough good things just maybe my mommy and daddy would love me and not hurt me. I became very self-sufficient. I can do it! I will be the best helper and just maybe my mommy won't hit me today. I will help daddy with the garden and then just maybe he won't have time to get drunk and hurt me. Just maybe!

My mask of fear was always with me hiding behind any other mask I had put on. I remember begging my mommy and daddy not to hurt me. I just wanted one day when I could be a happy little girl. I drug around the mask of insecurity every day wondering when my parents would send me away. Almost every day either my mommy or daddy would say we are going to send you away if you don't behave.

Early on I learned to control and hide my anger. I often thought what does my mask of anger look like but I am pretty sure it was a picture of a little girl that was hiding and crying, pleading not to be hurt again. Or maybe it was the little girl with a knife or baseball bat in her hand to protect herself.

As I got older I thought if I got fat daddy wouldn't like me but I didn't like myself either so I resorted to the mask of bulimia. At one point I became very anorexia to the point of losing forty pounds in one month. I begin to work at a very early age so I could have money to buy my diet pills. I became addicted to the point if I gained one pound I would increase the amount of pills I took that day or eat and then make myself throw up. I had put on the mask of control. I needed to be in control of something in my life. I became a people pleaser but inside of me was a little girl that was dealing with major depression, insecurity, thoughts of suicide frequently and anger issues. Many other masks seemingly helped to hide the pain and help me to cope with the past. Or did they? In letting all of these masks take over, they became the only passengers left in my vehicle and I was on the road to destruction.

I am brokenhearted and crushed in spirit. Does that describe the state of your mind? Is there any reality in how you feel? I felt as if nobody really wanted to be around me. I did not measure up. I felt I was not worthy of love and deserved to be punished.

All of these masks became a covering of untold pain and caused me to feel unloved and worthless. It seems like when we are hurting everybody wants to fix us. But inside my head the pain is so deep. I feel like I will never be happy again. My life is over. I will be alone forever. No one wants damaged goods. So how do I keep from lying to myself and others? The truth is what I need the most when the hurt is the deepest is someone to walk with me, love me and not judge me. But I can't trust anyone who says they love me.

Using drugs to cope with the pain had no effect on healing the emotional pain; I just continued to increase the amount of the drugs until I was addicted. Masks seemed to provide some emotional protection for a little while. But the cost of wearing a mask is high, you don't feel the warmth of belonging, of being loved because others really do not know the real you. It always seemed like I was the outsider wherever I went. I didn't want to be noticed and withdrew into the darkness surrounding me.

THE SEXUAL ABUSE WAS MY SECRET, A SECRET OF LIES
THAT BOUND ME TO SILENCE FOR OVER FIFTY YEARS.
IT WAS A SECRET I KEPT BECAUSE I ASSUMED NO ONE
ELSE COULD HANDLE THE UGLY TRUTH.

What could possibly give me the courage to have hope and peace in the midst of the darkness of my life? When I remember how God's love can transform our thoughts and feelings, I want to trust Him; the key word being "want" because I failed constantly. Jesus paid the ultimate price for our freedom from the darkness. The prophet Isaiah paints a picture of the coming Messiah as "a man of sorrows." He can relate to your feelings of isolation and betrayal when your heart is breaking. But can I trust Him?

Still my heart cried out how can I love God and trust Him when He had the power to change or at least stop the abuse, yet chose not to intervene? Then I saw my Savior, Jesus, crying out to his Father. "My God, my God, why have you forsaken me?"

The word father stirs up images of my daddy, some were warm and secure, others so frightening, cold, and abusive. I just wanted to find a safe place to hide. So I begin to put on mask after mask, just trying to survive one day at a time. The mask of denial; this is really happening to some other little girl. I really am not present because if I were I couldn't face the pain of betrayal. I sometimes chose someone in school that I didn't like and pretended I was her.

I often wore the mask of suicide because the pain was so intolerable. I would lay wide awake after being sexually abused and ask God what would it be like to die? Would I feel pain or just go to sleep? Helpless. Powerless. Trapped. Without hope. So dirty. I felt like I never could be clean enough. It seemed like the smell of sex was with me always. The mask of cleanliness became an obsession. Everything about me had to be clean and in order. It was a method I used to be in control of my body and surroundings. Have you ever felt this way? God is loving you through the pain, drawing you near, living inside of you. He brings comfort in distress, peace when your heart is overwhelmed. He cleanses us from all that is dirty and vile.

Do you hear the cry of my heart? When all I say is "I'm fine. Wounded, I hide, denying my pain. I am unable to confront the terror of the night. Will you cast me aside or hurt me too? Listen, just listen to my heart. Don't try to fix the pain. Just walk with me and love me. Hide me in the shadow of your love. Keep me safe in the refuge of your arms. Turn my darkness into light. Cause my pain to flee and love me until I am set free. I will not always love you back because I am afraid of love.

I hungered for healing and peace but it has been a long process. While thirsting for an intimate relationship with Jesus, I had to want to heal, to lay down the many masks one by one and become real. I wanted an instant transformation, but denial kept me from facing issues. I had to decide to face whatever I had been avoiding and take baby steps towards recovery. Obviously, the drugs had to go because they were a mask that kept me from dealing with all of the other problems. When taking drugs you wake up and the problem is still there, and the cycle starts over again and again. Burying your head in the sand and pretending that nothing is wrong, will not make the problems disappear. The only way to get rid of emotional pain is to deal with it head on. No masks and no drugs. They only create more situations you have to deal with.

It was black and cold in my self-imprisoned walls. Climbing the wall to reach the top seemed impossible as the walls were slippery with all of my pent-up emotions. Why me? What did I ever do to deserve this pain? Drugs have kept me bound; I saw no way out of my self-imposed prison. Step into the valley with me. See the prisoners chained to the walls. They are victims of betrayal, of sexual abuse, anger, and so many other feelings that leave them defenseless and defeated. Today I tell myself I will never believe anyone who tells me they love me. Love hurts and I am so tired of hurting. Words like worthless, slut, stupid caused me to make many choices that led me into eating disorders, addictions, and relationships that created even more pain.

Fear raised its ugly head. What will people think if I take off the masks? Can I handle all the pain and emotions without my safe escape of hiding behind drugs? Can I face the pain, release the emotions, and not be overwhelmed with fear or depression? At this point I don't really know. Without the drugs there are days when I cry out for deliverance from the depression. Sometimes fear takes over and I am in the valley of despair looking up and finding no answer to the overwhelming pain that surrounds my life. It is on those days I put the masks back on and declare the lie that I am fine. It is on those days I think about getting the drugs again.

Fear will incapacitate you and you will not be able to move forward. Take off the mask of fear and throw it away. Burn it, trample on it, but do not pick it up again. Fear is simply false evidence appearing real. God's perfect love will cast out all fear if you call upon Him; that is if you can only trust him. He will replace the violence with healing, give you joy and peace in the midst of the storms. He will replace rejection with acceptance, isolation with His presence, and low self-esteem by giving you the power to be an overcomer. The power of evil around you is no match for the power of Jesus in you. You can daily exercise your authority over the enemy. God hears your prayers, knows your struggles, and still wants you to call on His name. He came that we might be made whole through Him. But I am not sure if I can trust him. Does he really love me, the broken me, the little girl that runs from love?

Where have you come from and where are you going? If you are like me you may have decided it's easier to keep the masks on and run from your problems, and sidestep accountability. Accountability is not just being responsible to someone; for we can still keep our masks on and not be trustworthy. It is a process of being honest and vulnerable for your actions to someone you can trust to speak the truth into your life; and when you mess up you must take responsibility for your actions.

What drives our fear of being vulnerable? For me, it is exposing that what I feel is unacceptable, the disgrace of being sexually abused. I define vulnerability as exposure of my deepest feelings and actions. What price do we pay by avoiding vulnerability? We become almost like robots, no feelings, good or bad. I liked being a robot but sometimes the wrong buttons got pushed. Then I would explode in a whirlwind of anger in the most inappropriate places and times. Or maybe I can be one of those transformer toys, where I can change into what I want to be. I think I want to be the 7 Weapons Bumblebee. Then I could sneak up on anyone who is hurting me and sting them. Then just fly away!

To feel is to be vulnerable. Vulnerability is taking off the masks and wondering will people like the real me. It takes courage and faith, but each time we become vulnerable and speak the truth, we become more aware of the freedom God gives us. It gives us a sense of determination to expose the horror of sexual abuse and sexual trafficking. Will we allow our abuse to be exposed that others might be set free from the terror of sexual abuse and trafficking? Will we be willing to shout it out that God delivers?

We have to take off our masks to feel emotions, and that makes us vulnerable. Vulnerability is an emotional disclosure, of our shame, anger, and pain. Feelings of raw emotions are disclosed for others to see. Vulnerability demands accountability and working through the process of forgiveness. It feels like going out on a very high limb and hearing it begin to crack and then I begin to fall. I grab ahold of another limb, afraid to let go. Is the risk worth it?

> Sheila Walsh wrote that liberty lies in facing our fears.
> Why do I shutter my heart? Why do I keep it closed on days when
> it seems about to break? Why can't I let go? Why can't I ask for
> help and admit that I am barely alive? I think if I voice it, I'd have
> to believe it, to hear all the sadness. I just cannot bear it. That's
> why I shutter my heart.

Today this is the way I feel. My heart is shuttered. You can't see the brokenness. You can only see what I allow you to see. I can't ask for help. What would people say if they knew I feel so out of control? So I keep my heart closed so it won't become more broken. It's so dark inside my heart and the pain seems so overwhelming. But I must not tell anyone, they will send me away. I will be okay or will I?

For my broken heart to be mended I had to start with realizing what kind of a woman I want to be. Underneath the masks, was there the desire to be courageous, to risk going beyond my comfort zone? Will the pain cause me to crawl back into the darkness and allow the sickening feelings of despair surround me day and night? Can I survive in a world of violence where children are being abused daily? My heart breaks each time I hear or read about children being sexually abused. Just recently I read an article in the newspaper about a homecare for children where at least six children from the age of two to six were sexually abused. My heart cries out, Why God, why? Innocent children damaged for life, and I want to seek revenge on the abusers even though I know that is God's responsibility not mine.

Eleanor Roosevelt said:
You gain strength, courage, and confidence by every experience in which you really stop to look fear in the face. You are able to say to yourself, "I lived through this horror, I can take the next step.

Is the risk worth it? Yes, it is. For once you expose your fear, you can walk in faith and healing. Hope gives us the strength to walk in faith. Fear is a powerful enemy, so we need a powerful ally to help us overcome our fears. Jesus understands our fears and gives us comfort and strength to overcome them. It's one step at a time. If we conquer our fear of rejection and emotional distress and it helps one child, one woman to realize they can stand up and be set free from sexual, physical, or emotional abuse, it is worth it. Do you want to be changed by the unconditional love of God who delivers and sets us free from all bondage? It is time to shout it out. Sexual abuse is sin, but it's not your fault.

Psalms 34:4 I sought the Lord, and He answered me, he delivered me from all my fears.

Points to meditate on:
1. Identify the masks you are still wearing.
2. Can you deal with replacing one mask a week by surrendering it to God?
3. Take a step of faith and be honest with yourself. Write down all the things God is asking you to deal with.
4. How does it make you feel when you are vulnerable?
5. Realize that your healing does not necessarily get microwaved, it may be a crockpot healing. Be vulnerable and accountable to someone you can trust that believes in you. Above all, be honest about what you are feeling.
6. How does your experiences with your earthly father or your abuser influence your perspective of God, the Father?
7. What is your greatest fear?

WHERE IS GOD IN THE PAIN?

God, can you hear a little girls' cry? Daddy no! Stop! You are hurting me. Mommy where are you? But I must not cry or make any noise for daddy has said he will hurt my sisters. My daddy was a mean drunk and the scars he placed on my body were nothing compared to the scars on my heart. Innocent childhood ripped away, destroyed in one moment of pleasure for my daddy. For me my life was forever changed as innocent blood was shed. Daddy and mommy had no regards to facing consequences for their child abuse actions. I can't tell anyone because Daddy says he will know and hurt my sisters. My mother says she will beat me until I can't talk or send me away.

Helpless, trapped, powerless with no answers to my questions. Have you ever felt that way? Perhaps these words describe your circumstances now, or at least your perception of the circumstances. Where was everyone when bad things happened to us? I felt so violated and had no one I could talk to. I couldn't tell my aunt, her husband was there with my father the first time the abuse happened. Every time I saw him I was so scared. He was my father's identical twin. Would he also abuse me if he got the chance?

My aunt loved God but I couldn't understand why she said God knew what had happened. I had never told her even though we were close. If He did know how could he allow evil things to happen to children? Is it God's purpose for us to suffer pain? Have you ever wondered why you were born? I cried out to God in the days and months and even years after the abuse. God did your heart break like mine did on that morning when my father molested me? Did you weep as I laid in my bed crying? Did you know the day he first raped me? Did you see me when I was locked in the dark closet for hours because I fought back? Did you see the look on my mother's face when she said it was better that he was messing with me than her? I really cannot understand a god who doesn't protect innocent children. I find it hard to believe you love me but I am trying to trust you.

God, where were you when I was knocked down the stairs because I fought back and couldn't go to school for almost two weeks? I know you knew that I lied to the counselor when she asked me what happened. I couldn't tell her the truth because things would have gotten worse at home. I was really glad to get back to school because for the most part I felt safe there.

We ask the question why do bad things happen, but what about asking the question, God what do you want to accomplish in my life? The bottom line is we are not to depend upon what we think or our ability to answer the why questions. Don't think God isn't listening. He is answering requests you are not even making. Your prayers move God to change the circumstances; but God isn't under any obligation to answer our questions. If we looked at the life of Job, we see that God remained silent until the last few chapters before He spoke to Job. Did God love Job any less when he didn't immediately answer Job and bless him?

You may be asking, if God loves me, why am I struggling with pain from my past? Why can't I just let it go as so many good meaning Christians say if you tell them about your struggles? If God loves me, why has He allowed so much hurt in my life? Do I have the right to question God's plan for my life? Why did He allow my family to be broken by adultery, alcohol, and physical, sexual and emotional abuse? Why didn't He prevent the pain I brought on myself? The only answer I can give you about all the why questions we ask of God is that God gave mankind a choice in the Garden of Eden. Adam and Eve could have obeyed the one single commandment that God gave them, but they chose to disobey and sin entered into the garden. From that day forth we were born into sin and shaped into iniquity.

Do we have enough insight to understand why we ask all the why questions? I believe that God set life up this way as a test of our faith. Will we love Him in the midst of the fiery trials or will we reject His intervention of unconditional love in our lives because of the pain we are facing?

Ruth Bell Graham, wife of evangelist Billy Graham, put it so beautifully when she wrote the following:

I lay my "whys?
Before your cross
In worship kneeling
My mind beyond all hope,
My heart beyond all feeling:
And worshipping,
Realize that,
In knowing you,
I don't need a "why?"

Why did Jesus die for us? Why did He go to the cross, the sinless Son of God'? Simply because of His great love for each of us. How can I continue to ask "why?" when Jesus paid the ultimate price for my freedom and healing? But there are still days I cry out to God, "Why!" Why am I still here? Why did you stop me from taking that handful of pills? I have been running for so long with no peace. I am so tired. Allow me to see if you are real. The darkness was overwhelming as I picked up the bottle of pills; then God let me see he loved me even though he did not approve of my choices and desire to end my life. He spoke to my heart in that moment, I love you just as you are. Trust me with every part of your life. Then he wrapped me in his arms and simply held me and loved me. He said, I have a plan for your life.

God's plan for you and me is nothing short of a new heart. The seed of Jesus' love has been planted, but what will we do with it? Now it is our choice. Will we believe that we are chosen by God, loved just as we are, and called to be children of God?

> Proverbs 3:5 states: Trust in the Lord with all your heart and lean
> not unto your own understanding.

God wants us to trust no matter what the circumstances are, whether we caused them or someone whom we loved betrayed us. Not once does God say, Worry about it or figure it out. But over and over, the Bible clearly says "Trust God." Does God know how hard it is for me to just trust Him?

It is in the moments when we cannot understand we must choose to trust God enough that we can share our fears, feelings, and ask for help. God reaches out to rescue us no matter what problems we are struggling with. You may be looking for answers because you're in a faltering marriage, an abusive relationship, had an abortion, depressed or numerous other situations. God still loves you. His desire was not for us to suffer. Even today God wants to heal your hurts, and redeem your pain. Your part is to seek God, call upon Him, be obedient and believe that He is able to heal all your wounds. As we begin to surrender to God, He redeems us from our past, give us hope, and uses our scars to help others.

You may be thinking it is easy but it isn't. I still struggle with issues that stem from years of sexual abuse and rape. My heart breaks every time I hear of a child being abused. For when all you can see is too difficult for you to comprehend or move forward, all God sees is how much He loves you and me.

IT HAS BEEN SO DIFFICULT TO WRAP MY MIND AROUND THE FACT THAT GOD LOVES ME WITHOUT MY HAVING TO PERFORM IN A CERTAIN WAY OR DO NUMEROUS ACTS OF MINISTRY.

He places no conditions on our redemption except that we must receive the sacrificial gift of salvation provided to us by the death of His son, Jesus. For years I functioned in all types of ministry wanting God to love me. But it wasn't enough! I couldn't really believe He loved me! I needed to surrender all the pain to Him and just trust Him moment by moment. Will God release me from the pain and from the terror of the abuse? What does he require of me? God simply requires surrender and obedience. Just say yes!

Take a moment to picture this scene. Abraham finally has his promised son only for God to command him to sacrifice that son. Does Abraham stop and begin to ask God why He would ask him to sacrifice his only son? No, he doesn't. We see Abraham preparing the altar, we see Abraham clench his teeth, place his son upon the altar and tie him there, then lift the knife in the air ready to obey God. His heart is breaking as he tries to control his anguish but he did not ask God why. Suddenly he hears a voice from heaven telling him not to touch his son. The Lord provided a ram for the sacrifice. Abraham could have asked God all kinds of why questions but he simply obeyed and believed that God would provide a lamb. God's promise and love intervened and a ram was provided for the sacrifice.

Is it too much for us to make the same choice to obey and have faith that God can heal our wounds? The trial you and I are facing today is not too difficult for God to handle. We must just trust and obey. God is able to intervene, break the chains of abuse, and set us free.

God is waiting for you to give Him the broken pieces of your life so that He can make something beautiful out of them. He has waited for me for fifty years to call upon Him for the healing I need. It took the love of one women willing to share her time to reach out and confront the issues in my life. I was broken but she reached out with unconditional love. I don't know what she saw in my life that she thought was worthwhile redeeming but I know she loved me.

God doesn't just want us to forget the things of the past, He wants us to use them to minister to others. God sends people to us who need to hear our stories and we must be ready to share. The question is will we expose our past that others might be healed? He has a purpose for your life and mine in spite of our pain. He releases us from our past and redeems our pain; but we must accept and acknowledge the circumstances that can't be changed, let go and move on.

Jesus becomes real to others when we tell our story, how God lifted us from the pit of hell, and set our feet on the solid rock and established a new life pathway. Shout it out. God's love delivers and sets us free!

> He is the glory and lifter of my head. "We overcome Satan by the blood of the Lamb and by the word of our testimony." Revelation 12:11

Brene Brown says "When we deny our stories, they define us. When we own our stories, we get to write the ending." The beginning and all the years in between defined me as a victim of abuse. The ending defines me as a women of God. I am a new creation of infinite worth. I am deeply loved, and complete in Christ. God has made me an original, one of a kind, really somebody!

Being real is what really matters. I often have asked myself will the real me stand up and introduce herself to the world? We cannot continue to pretend, put on our happy masks, and try to leave a good impression. We must speak the truth to ourselves first, and then to other women and children who are still being abused and told not to tell.

SHOUT IT OUT LOUD AND CLEAR! GOD DELIVERS!

Sometimes we cannot do it alone, we need someone to come along and stand beside us. Keeping the poisonous thoughts bottled up inside of us only means that it continually eats away at us. We need the confidence that things can change and we can be restored and made whole.

Let's look briefly at the story of Jacob found in Genesis 32: 22-31. Jacob was fearful as he approached where his hostile brother Esau lived. God sent angels to assure Jacob that He was with him. He wasn't sure that Esau would greet him and his family with open arms or would he be greeted with violence because of his deception. He felt unworthy and prayed for God's protection and deliverance. He stated the ultimate purpose for requesting God's protection, was that he was to fulfil God's covenant purpose in his life. As Jacob wrestled with God for the promised blessing, God disabled Jacob's hip. Jacob could no longer walk in his own strength but must rely entirely on God. We must reach that place where we rely on God alone. I can't do it alone and neither will you be able to do it alone.

My scars and yours are beautiful to God. You can find peace and purpose in the hurts of your past but you must be real. Peel off every mask and let God heal your pain. I compare taking off a mask like peeling an onion, layer by layer. It is painful and you will cry. Not every page in our lives will have a happy ending, but the victory will be sweeter because of the struggle. If you have been sexually, physically, or emotionally abused it is a process to obtain complete freedom from the past.

Today, I declare that I am not what happened to me, I am what I have determined to become. Healing is not about finding all the right answers, it's letting go and being the right person equipped by God to reach out to love other suffering women and children through their pain.

What does God write on the whiteboard about your past? You are chosen, loved, healed by His stripes, holy, beautiful, and special. If God can take an old pile of dried up bones, cause them to rise up into a mighty army, He can surely take the broken pieces of our lives and transform us into mighty warriors to stand against abuse of any kind.

Issues to think upon:
1. What "Why" questions are you asking?
2. What are your thoughts on Ruth Bell Graham' statement, "I lay my "whys" before your cross?
3. Identify how you can use your past to help others

Obstacles

For every hill I've had to climb
For every stone that bruised my feet
For all the blood and sweat and grime
My heart sings, but a grateful song.
These were the things that made me strong.

For all the heartaches and the tears
For all the anguish and pain
For gloomy days, my fruitless years
And for the hopes that lived in vain
I do give thanks, for now I know
Those were the things that made me grow.

Tis not the softer things of life
Which stimulate our will to survive,
But bleak adversity and strive
Do most to keep our will alive.
Over rose strewn paths the weaklings creep
But brave hearts dare to climb the steep.

Author Unknown

WILL YOU LISTEN TO MY STORY?

The Bud

And the day came when the risk to remain
Tight in a bud was more painful
Than the risk it took to blossom.
Author Unknown

Do you remember those days you sat around a campfire eating hot dogs and s'mores, singing campfire songs? Soon everyone began to tell stories, some were probably true, and others made up. I loved to listen to the stories and try to imagine what it would be like to have close family relationships like my friends did. They told of the fun things that happened in their lives, and the things that made them sad. I just sat and listened. The only story I could think of was the day I made a chocolate cake for our picnic but left it at home. When we arrived back at the farm, there was a skunk sitting on the kitchen table enjoying that cake. Well, we all know that if you scare a skunk, it's going to be pretty stinky for a while. As I watched that skunk eating the cake I had worked so hard to make, I thought about how stinky my life was but I didn't have anything to spray on those who were abusing me.

Many times sitting at a table listening to my friends and others talk, seemingly comfortable and at ease, I often wonder would they really like me if I told them my story? Why does it seem so easy for everyone else to fit in? Will I ever feel like I don't have to accomplish so much to be acceptable? Most of them only know me superficially. Shame and guilt kept me bound and I asked myself will I ever be free of old memories and shame. Can I believe like the woman in Mark 5:25-35 did when she heard about Jesus?

Let's just take a brief look at the woman in Mark 5:25-35; a woman who had been subject to bleeding for twelve years. She had suffered a great deal under the care of many doctors and had spent all she had, yet instead of getting better she grew worse. The woman is desperate. When she heard about Jesus, she came up behind him in the crowd and touched His cloak, because she thought, "If I just touch His clothes, I will be healed." Immediately her bleeding stopped and she felt in her body that she was freed from her suffering. Jesus said to her, "Daughter, your faith has healed you, go in peace and be freed from your suffering."

I wish I had that kind of crazy faith, to just believe, reach out and touch the hem of Jesus garments. It seems like I can always believe for other people but it is a different story when I pray for myself. Her part in the healing was very small. All she did was reach out and touch the hem of His garment. Healing begins when we do something, when we reach out, and when we take a step of faith. I can't heal my body, or erase the bad things that happened to me or change the decisions I made. But God can. Just because He loves us. Is my faith strong enough to reach out and just be delivered? Or do I believe only for short term relief; followed by more depressive thinking that I am not good enough.

When we reach a point where we are addicted to food, drugs, alcohol, work, or anything else that we think we can control; these things become like poison to us. We develop toxic relationships and we are not able to feel spontaneous emotions. For many years I walked in these types of toxic behaviors, not knowing that real love could change my life. I needed to reach out and to develop the same kind of faith this woman displayed. I call it crazy faith, faith that lets nothing or anyone hinder their healing. But would God honor that kind of faith in my life? Yes, because He loves me!

Jesus is just as interested in our needs as He was in this woman's need many years ago. Whatever your situation, whatever your problem, He is ready to help you. The bigger the walls, the more hopeless the situation seems, God still cares and loves you unconditionally. Have you waited twelve years or more for God's healing? I waited fifty years in silence before I reached out for help. He is ready to touch your life with power, deliverance, and healing.

You are not just a sexually abused child, you are so much more. Why are we so insecure and afraid to open up? We are women not children and we have the power to stand and be recognized as women of God. If one word could become a reality in your life, what would it be? I would chose the words loved and accepted. That's not just one word is it? I always wanted to feel accepted and loved, not for what I could do or even be but just because I am me. The reality was I believed for a long time I had to earn acceptance from God. God begin to show me that I associated my performance with my acceptability. From the time I was a little girl I was accepted only if I did exactly what my mother or father wanted me to do. I have struggled for many years with trusting the truth that God loved me and accepted me. We are accepted not because of what we do or who we are but because God loves us with an everlasting love.

Stories have impact, and we all have baskets filled to the brim and running over with life lessons. But the question remains, are we willing to share our stories? Can we take off the masks enough to be authentic? It is a difficult process as the masks for some of us have been in place for many years. Over fifty years I never spoke of the sexual abuse, afraid of being rejected, scorned, unable to face the betrayal of my father and mother. Fear caused me to be quiet and suffer in silence. To this day I still have difficult talking about the abuse, the silence that was demanded of me, and how it made me feel. It is time to shout out that God delivers!

We develop behavior patterns that make us feel good for the short period of time we are supposedly in control. I became a person who learned how to perform according to the demands of my mother and father. My childhood was full of painful experiences. Instead of learning how to play, laugh, running and being a joyful child I lived in fear. No one ever said to me I am proud of you. Keep up the good work. You are special. Because of this I became very disconnected from my family, and from sharing any emotional experiences such as joy, excitement, anger, or crying. My reality of family life was totally distorted. I wept as I listened to my baby sister as she shared memories of our family life. For so many years there was no contact between us. As I spoke to her about God, she said one of the greatest treasures she has is the Bible I gave her when she was around thirteen. We both wanted a family that would love us.

Friends may desert us, family members reject us, but God will never abandon us. In place of shame, rejection, fear and condemnation, our most significant act of spiritual warfare is choosing to know who we are in God. It's time to change the channel or stop driving down the same road, staring in the rearview mirror. It's time to take a step of faith and reach out for assistance. I made that choice three years ago when I was confronted about the abuse. Even then, I had much difficulty in revealing the circumstances surrounding my childhood. It was an interruption of love that changed my perspective on being willing to share my story.

My heart aches each time I hear about a woman or child being abused. Recently I read in the news that teachers are having sex with children in schools, a gym teacher was charged with 30 counts of statutory rape, and a woman with children is dating a convicted child molester and allowing him to be with her children alone. Priests and other religious leaders are sexually abusing children. Up to 7% of all middle and high school students are targets of sexual abuse from someone in authority or working in the school system. Is it enough to feel sorrowful about what is happening to our children, or is it time to be a voice for the innocent?

Life for most of us is constant change; learning to let go and trust again is a major process for abused children. We cannot reverse what has happened to us, but we can change the outcome by changing our response to trials. Change is a matter of choice, we do our part and God definitely will do His part. If you have always been a negative person, begin to change how you think. Then begin to speak positive things instead of the negative. Believe me that isn't easy! I am quick to speak and believe the negative things and give up easily. But I am blessed with women of God in my life who are very positive and don't hesitate to encourage me not to be negative. They haven't given up on me yet!

> Acknowledge the pain like Job did.
> Job 7:11
> "Therefore I will not keep silent; I will speak out in the anguish of
> my spirit. I will complain in the bitterest of my soul."

It sounds easy when I read the book of Job but I know it hasn't been easy for me. When I begin to deal with the issues concerning the sexual abuse, the nightmares and flashbacks began. I had difficulty sleeping, and fear raised its ugly head saying you can't do this. I became more and more addicted to prescription drugs in order to cope with the pain. But healing comes with being brave enough to take off the masks and reveal the truth. No one loves us or offers healing like God does. Acknowledge your pain. No matter what others have said, your pain is valid. No pain is too small or too large that God can't handle it. God keeps pouring His love into our hearts, an unconditional inexhaustible love to heal our wounds. He wants to take your brokenness, interrupt your life with his unconditional love and continue to love you through the pain.

No night is too long, no battle to hard with Jesus beside you. No situation is too hopeless; there are no chains too strong that they can't be broken. The battle is not ours alone, we have Jesus by our side.

As I reflect on my life when I was child, I realized I had no control over the situation. Physical, emotional, and sexual abuse were a part of my life from the day I turned five. There was no one who listened to my story or made an attempt to change the circumstances. Actually the physical abuse started before I was two years old. How does a young child cope with such tragic situations? Many children never recover from the type of abuse that was afflicted on me at such an early age.

As I grew older I realized I was broken and like Humpty Dumpty I didn't know if all the broken pieces could be put back together. Sadly, I didn't know if all the pieces were even available, so for a long time I went limping through life, pretending I was okay. Instead of seeking healing from God, I ignored the pain and confusion, unable to deal with all the emotions. But the pain never really heals by ignoring it or putting on one of those masks that says, "I am fine and don't ask me again." While we may never be "good as new;" we can receive emotional healing here on earth. It is a process but we must quit ignoring the truth and begin to deal with our past hurts, one step at a time. And then leave them in the past. It is time to reach for those things that are ahead, peace, love, forgiveness, and allowing God to complete his work in our lives.

Running into walls was a part of my life until I quit ignoring the truth. The walls were massive consisting of sickness, abuse, darkness, depression, and fear which surrounded me. It seemed like the walls enclosed me with a sense of danger on all sides, and there was no escape. I sought love in all the wrong places and from all the wrong people. Sometimes I just didn't think anyone could love me. Because of the physical and sexual abuse, I lived with the belief and fear that there had to be a big letter "A" on my forehead, meaning go ahead and abuse me.

For years I could not see past the pain and destruction in my life. The wall of self-denial was in place hiding my shame. It seemed like the shame encircled me in a wall of bricks, allowing no one else to touch or reach me. I just knew I could not allow anyone to see my pain and try to comfort me. I never realized how shame crushes a child's natural exuberance, their curiosity, and their desire to feel strong enough to assert themselves and resist sexual advances.

As I became older, most of the time I resisted any expressions of love due to fear of the price I would have to pay to be loved. It took a long time for me to learn to allow people to hug me. I believe God put me in a church where hugs are a normal part of the service. That's just like God as he wants us to confront the pain and be healed. It was difficult at first. As a child I almost always told people who wanted to hug me, "Don't touch me!"

As a child that was embarrassed of her family, I often expressed the feeling of never really being joyful and free to be a child. I had intense feelings of inadequacy and extreme emotional thoughts of being unlovable. There came a time after being sexually molested for years that all I felt was ashamed of my family and myself because sometimes I felt physical pleasure. My heart cried out, how can this be?

Why would anyone else love me if my parents didn't? The most difficult journey is to go back to the place where the pain began. But that is where we must begin, on that first day of the abuse. In looking back to that day I was first molested, I realize my life was forever changed. For years I would never wear anything that was red or had red in it. My father gave me two dresses that day, one that was red and the other a red plaid.

Let me share with you just a little part of my story right now. My story is filled with pain as I was molested at the age of five by my father. The molestation continued throughout the following years increasing until the day came when my father raped me. I was molested by two of my brothers during that period of time also.

My mother did not protect me, and her words when I spoke to her of the abuse still linger in my mind to this day. Why would a mother not only ignore the abuse her daughter is receiving but actually say that it is okay for her father to abuse her? We must remember that words do more than convey messages. The power of our words can actually destroy one's spirit, and even lead to hatred and violence. Even today those words linger in my mind and I cannot even begin to understand why she said them.

Proverbs 18:21 states that the tongue has the power of life and death. Words can heal or kill, build or destroy. What happened behind closed doors when we were children is often not an acceptable role model. No matter what our age and regardless of how painful our past has been, it's wrong to think that God allows words to be used to wound others deeply.

I urge you to listen to any child that speaks to you of abuse and check it out. I perceived myself as unclean, worthless and all alone. It was my father's and my secret never to be spoken out loud. I wore many masks as a child and teenager, never letting anyone know my secret. School was a way of escape but I always had to return home. My heart aches when I think that at some point the molestation begin to feel good. God made us to be sexual beings but not to be used and abused. Many times during the years my greatest desire was to just die; but God kept me for this time of healing.

For years I could not see past the pain and destruction in my life. The wall of self-denial became a mask hiding my shame; shame that was enclosed in a wall of bricks, allowing me to wallow in self-pity and pain. I wore the mask of rejection; I knew I was unlovable; especially since my mother and father never loved me. Why would anyone else love me if my parents didn't? The most difficult journey is to go back to the place where the pain began but that is where we must start for the healing to begin.

Have you ever considered the thought that God doesn't see any value in your life because of what happened to you? Have you looked in the mirror and wished you didn't look like either one of your parents? Have you ever heard the words, I don't want you? You are worthless and will never amount to anything. I wish you had never been born. Unwanted! That was me!

We want to connect with another person, reach out, touch, and be loved. But when that link with another person is violated by any type of abuse, we withdraw and retreat into a world of silence, pain, and isolation. I was afraid to connect for I knew connection brought pain and rejection.

Through it all Jesus still loved me. He knows my abusive past, my past addictions, and still loves me. Do you feel loved? Regardless of your past, your imperfections, you are chosen by God for a task that perfectly fits your talents.

No one loves us or offers healing like God does. Perhaps it is time for you to acknowledge the pain like Job did in Job 7:11. "Therefore I will not keep silent; I will speak out in the anguish of my spirit. I will complain in the bitterness of my soul." Healing comes with being courageous enough to reveal the truth."

Stepping out into the unknown can leave us terrified when no one believes us. What about the children who never speak of their abuse, children who have been so traumatized as early as three years old? Can we just walk away and do nothing? I took care of a woman who had been sexually assaulted as a child of three. She never spoke again except to swear and say the word no. She wouldn't allow me to touch her even though she always looked like she wanted a hug when I hugged her roommate. As I worked with her she finally came to me for a hug and began to shake the hands of people at church. My heart broke the first time she actually wanted a hug and responded to others who offered her love. It is being loved that changes us and breaks the barriers we have established in our lives. Her social worker could not understand how I was able to reach her, but then I never had told her I was sexually abused at an early age. I don't want to come to the end of my life just saying I will be safer if I don't speak out for the children and women who are being abused.

The masks I have worn over the years didn't keep me safe. Night after night I woke up screaming, and shaking from the nightmares. I could not sleep in a house without a light on. All the walls I had built did not keep me safe from being sexually abused again and again, nor did they keep away the memories of the heartache from the abuse.

2 Samuel 13:12-14 tells of a story that didn't have a happy ending. We meet Tamar, the virgin daughter of King David. Her half-brother desired her, ordered everyone out of his home and asked Tamar to come to him in the bedroom. She obeyed. She knew the loss of her virginity meant she would never marry. But he overpowered her and raped her. Violated and ashamed, she lost everything. She was broken, hopeless, and alone. Like Tamar, I was overcome by my abusers and lived in depression and silence for many years.

What about you? Do you have a memory that breaks your heart? Perhaps your wound is old, part of you is broken; and you are angry and bitter. Part of you wants to cry, and another part of you wants to fight. You are left with a decision. Will you continue to allow the pain of the past to control your life, keep all your masks on or will you allow the hole in your heart to be healed?

Today I know that God can take the broken pieces of my life and make all things new. He heals the brokenhearted and restores unto us joy. Is healing needed in your life? God can heal all your wounds; He specializes in healing His children. In place of your greatest shame, step out in an act of faith and choose to believe that God loves you. I began to declare that God loves me, even with all the baggage, He still loves me.

The Spirit of the living God and his unconditional love is what is setting me free. My scars and tears are beautiful to Him. You can find that same peace, purpose and deliverance. You will need to take the masks off, one by one. It will not necessarily be easy because we are so used to hiding our feelings and reactions to pain. Not every page in our life has a happy ending. The victory will be sweeter because of the struggle. God delights in showing us mercy and giving us peace.

When you are in a very dark place, have you ever considered that perhaps the darkness is only the shadow of God's hand shielding you from greater danger? When we go through trials which wound us so deeply, and we cannot talk about it, have you ever asked God what He is trying to teach you?

Psalms 91:1&4 reads as follows; "He who dwells in the shelter of the Most High will rest in the shadow of the Almighty. He will cover you with His feathers, and under His wings you will find refuge."

We are His! He wants us to be totally restored. He speaks the following words to us, "Do not fear for I have redeemed you." Run to Him for healing and restoration. He is our redeemer, the one who liberates us. God knew there was a time that I would seek Him. He knew the day I would quit playing the blame game, and release my shame to Him. The price was already paid, the blood of the Lamb of God was shed.

God opened the prison doors of my heart, and then He begin to teach me to walk in freedom and deliverance. Every chain, every bondage needs to be broken. Our God changes caterpillars into beautiful butterflies, sand into pearls, coal into diamonds, using time and pressure. He desires to break every chain that has us bound.

His love, is not dependent upon my past, nor even my behavior. I cling to the promise that perfect love casts out all fear. I have been chosen, loved, and accepted by God because of what Christ did on the cross. By the word of my testimony and the blood of the Lamb, I will seek to break all bondage. Satan I put you on the alert, all bondage must go. The walls must come tumbling down, fear banished, shackles broken, no control will be yours. Satan, you are the destroyer but freedom is mine as I hold fast to the hand of God. Truth triumphs, fear will face faith, and victory is mine for I know God interrupted my broken life with His unconditional love. I will shout it out; God loves, delivers and sets us free from all bondage.

Points to consider:
1. Will you tell your story?
2. Will you identify the brokenness in your life?
3. How do you feel about yourself today?
4. Will you let God's love change your li

Reflections

When you look in the mirror, who do you see?
Do you see evil, pain and suffering?
Or do you see me?

When you look in the mirror, who do you see?
Do you see anger, jealousy, and envy?
Or do you see me?

When you look in the mirror, who do you see?
Do you see failure, disappointment, and pity?
Or do you see me?

When you look in the mirror, who do you see?
Do you see love, strength, and beauty?
That is me!

Remember that you are always a reflection of me.
When you look in the mirror, look at me,
and I will show you who you are to me.
Author: Amy Bates

What do you see when you look in the mirror? Do you see only brokenness or do you see a woman who is loved by the unconditional love of an Almighty God? Do you see God in you when you look in a mirror or do you only see the destruction of the abuse? Do you see joy and peace, or only sadness?

Jean Anouilh says:
"Our entire life consists ultimately in accepting ourselves as we are."

Questions to think about.
1. Who are you a reflection of and why?
2. Can you identify who loves you and why?
3. Will you share your reflection of who you are with another hurting woman or child?
4. Identify your strengths and weaknesses.

SMILING BROKEN HEARTS

I see your smiling faces even while
Your mask covers the pain of abuse
My heart reaches to connect with yours
Your pain becomes mine as I touch you
The I cry for your loss of innocence
Our tears mingle, our hearts are entwined
I hold you close, my heart aches, then breaks.

Your pain becomes mine, and then I weep
Trying to reach out and heal your deepest wounds
But we are both broken, inside and out
Hearts crying out for the release of the pain
You see me as I see you, smiling on the outside
But living with a shattered heart
Questioning, "Where are you God?"

God's love breaks the barriers, gives us victory
As our tears are captured in His hands
Pain is erased as we release it to God
We embrace each other, reaching out
To touch the lives of all our sisters
Declaring the victory that is ours to share
As His touch heals and breaks down the barriers.

ADVERSITY DOESN'T DEFINE YOU

Arthur Golden says that adversity is like a strong wind. It tears away from us all but the things that cannot be torn, so that we see ourselves as we really are.

I looked deep into my heart this morning and asked myself, how do I see myself as a child? I know that I liked to pretend I was a mother, cooking and taking care of my baby. My father had bought me a three foot doll when I was three years old, a doll house, and baking and kitchen set. The doll walked, talked, cried and could be fed with her little bottle. Everywhere I went the doll was with me. I watched my mother as she took care of my brother and sister. My baby got a bath, fed, and her clothes changed when my little sister did.

Then it happened. At the age of five my whole world seemed to crumble. There was danger all around me. I no longer felt safe or wanted to play with my doll, cook and make meals for her. At times I would try to do the things my daddy had done to me to my doll. After being sexually abused at the age of five the things that were important to me, love, family, playing and happiness were all torn from me.

I was too young to know how to change my circumstances. If you want to overcome adversity you have to focus on the positive. My world was turned upside down. Who will listen even if I have the courage to tell what happened? I didn't understand, I only knew that what had happened was bad and hurt. I was so afraid of my daddy now and didn't want to be around him. Daddy said you can't tell anyone. You know I love you. You are my special little girl. I didn't feel special anymore. I was now afraid of my daddy and most of the time I tried to run away from him crying and screaming, no, Daddy, don't touch me!

I was never the same trusting little girl again. The strong winds of adversity may very well hold you back, toss you around like a rag doll, but then again adverse conditions can make you stronger. It all depends upon how you respond. I continued to fight for the strength to be more than what my family was, to succeed by obtaining an education, looking towards the future. Sometimes life seemed to be completely overwhelming. The only things that occupied my mind were stressful situations. They felt like a heavy burden, weighing me down, sapping all of my energy to fight. I find myself obsessing about all the negative situations in my life. Jean Anouilh says, "Our entire life consists ultimately in accepting ourselves as we are." I didn't like me and didn't want to accept who I was.

When adverse situations surround you and seem to be closing in on you, it is then you need to hold on. A friend of mine uses the illustration her mother taught her. Just tie a knot in the end of the rope and hang on, keeping your eyes on God. The end of the rope is the beginning of God's doorstop. I couldn't open the door for there wasn't any doorknob. Can you anticipate coming face to face with all the impossibilities and letting them go, one by one?

Can we allow God to fight our battles? He says when you pass through the waters he will be with you. Do not focus on the absence of problems in your life. This is an unrealistic goal, since we live in a world full of violence and stress. We will go thru many hardships but God has promised he will bring us through if we trust him. Trust was not easy for me. I wanted immediate change and healing.

In the quietness of the morning hour I sit before God, and reflect on how God has a purpose and desires to take my broken dreams and heal my mind. In the stillness I find forgiveness as I release my fears and anger to the Lord. I know I must forgive my abusers but it is so difficult.

Just recently I finally had a breakthrough and was able to forgive my mother and myself. When my mother was on her death bed she told me she loved me. I always wanted my mother to tell me she loved me. I reacted in anger and as I walked out of her room, the Holy Spirit spoke to my heart. I heard him clearly say I brought her back to tell you that she loves you. My child that is how much I love you.

It is time to shout it out that God delivers, sets us free, and heals the broken places. The chains of sexual abuse are being broken, one by one.

Perhaps it is time for you to acknowledge your pain and throw away the masks you have been wearing. It doesn't matter what others have said, your pain is valid. No pain is too small or too large that God can't handle it. All adversities have consequences but we can change the way we think about them. Is it simple? God has never promised that it would be easy only that He would walk with us.

Adversity comes in many ways, sidetracking us from the truth. We are like a broken toy but we can be fixed. At one time or even many times we've been hurt, betrayed, left out, and abused. We've been conditioned to put on a smile and pretend we are not broken. The problem is broken things don't fix themselves. We simply exist. We can't trust people who are supposed to love and protect us. We seek attention and affection, and then realize that it is almost always followed by sexual demands.

We don't have control over our body, other people's needs come ahead of ours. We see danger all around us, and know that we are not in complete control. Someone else has the final word. We ignore the pain, develop many stress related habits, become addicted to drugs, alcohol, food, self-abuse and the pain never ends. We just keep on multiplying, and exploding in destructive behaviors. We may attend support group meetings, seek extensive counseling, and attend conferences, but still never receive complete healing. Only God can erase the past, and make us whole.

Adversity is a part of everyone's life. Pain and death are a part of life. To reject them even if it was possible is to reject life itself. Many sexually abused children reject anything that relates to what is happening to them and turn to alternate life-styles where they feel safe.

Healing for me began when I began to release my trampled on broken heart to God. I begin to declare that God loved me, and even with all the baggage, He still loved me. It was an incredible awakening when I accepted that fact. God's type of love seeks the highest good for each one of us. It is the most powerful weapon of restoration and available to all who seek Him. His love is unconditional and never, not even once does He tell us not to speak of it. I couldn't love myself but God still loved me.

Look at 2 Samuel 13:11, and see what happened to Tamar. When she took bread to her brother to eat, he grabbed her and said, come to bed with me, my sister. She cried out no, don't force me! Don't do this wicked thing. What about me? Where could I get rid of my disgrace? And what about you? You would be like one of the wicked fools in Israel! He refused to listen to her, and since he was stronger than her he raped her.

Here in the Bible we see the words that are spoken to every woman and child that have been sexually abused or raped. Be quiet for now. Don't take this thing to heart. Violated and ashamed, she lost everything. Her brothers' horrific act left her broken, alone, and hopeless. Do you feel that way?

Like Tamar, I was overpowered by my abusers and lived in depression and silence for many years. Now I know that God makes all things new. He heals the brokenhearted and restores unto us joy.

> Isaiah 53:4-5
> Surely he took up our pain, and bore our suffering, yet we consid-
> ered him punished by God, stricken by him and afflicted. But He
> was pierced for our transgressions, He was crushed for our inequi-
> ties; the punishment that brought us peace was on him, and by his
> wounds we are healed.

When you respond positively and constructively to your biggest challenges, the qualities of strength and courage emerge from deep inside of you. Of course since we are human, it is very easy to get caught up in self-pity and the unfairness of life. As a child I was frightened, didn't know how to respond or even under-stand what was happening. I only knew betrayal and pain.

Isaiah wrote, "No weapon formed against you (or me) will prosper and every tongue which rises against you in judgment you shall condemn. This is the heritage of the servants of God, and their righteousness is from me, says the Lord." Isaiah 54:17

The last part of this message from Isaiah says that God will condemn the voices of darkness that rise up to condemn us. The question is are we willing to take off the masks and begin the process of healing we so desperately need? What will you do with your scars, scars that have kept you chained to the past? Will you release your memories, your pain to God and let Him heal and deliver you?

You have to settle in your mind that your need is spiritual; no drugs, no alcohol, no human and no amount of money can meet your need. Counselors, psychiatrists, and doctors, can help you to a certain extent but God can deliver you. Even after extensive counseling for a year, and being a counselor I was not delivered from the pain of the sexual abuse.

We want to be in control because we didn't have any control when we were sexually abused or raped; but God demands that we surrender to Him. He has known all along your deepest needs and wounds, heard the deep groans of your soul. He is only asking for you to be real and admit that you need Him.

> Psalms 61; 1-3
> Hear my cry, God, listen to my prayer, from the ends of the earth I will call to you. I call as my heart grows faint. Lead me to the rock that is higher than I. For you have been my refuge, a strong tower against the foe.

Let's just take a minute to look at how Paul and Silas handled adversity. In Acts 16:16-40 we see Paul and Silas on their way to a place of prayer. The next thing we see is a slave girl, known for being a psychic. She made a lot of money for the people who owned her. She started following Paul and Silas around yelling out that these men are working for the most High God. They are speaking of salvation. She continued this for many days, harassing Paul and Silas as they went about doing the work of the Lord. Finally Paul was fed up with her, turned and commanded the spirit that possessed her to leave her alone.

When her owners realized what had happened, and they could no longer exploit her and receive money from her; they went after Paul and Silas. They roughed them up and dragged them into the market place, where the police arrested them, took them to court proclaiming that they were dangerous Jewish agitators. By this time the crowd had turned into a restless mob who were out for blood.

The judges ruled against Paul and Silas, ripped their clothes off and ordered a public beating. They then threw them into prison, ordering the jail keeper to put them under heavy protection so there would be no chance of escape. Because the jailor feared for his position, he threw them into the maximum security cell, clamping leg irons on them so they could not escape.

It's interesting to view how Paul and Silas in the midst of this adversity responded. About midnight when most people would be sleeping, Paul and Silas were praying. Picture this scene, irons around their legs, praying out loud, not silently, so that the other prisoners could not hear them. In the midst of this adverse situation they were singing and praying. I can almost hearing them singing, "Every praise belongs to God." The other prisoners couldn't believe what they were hearing. Then, without a warning, a huge earthquake passed through. The jailhouse was battered, every door flew open, and all the prisoners were loosed.

The jailor was frightened as he observed that all the doors on the cells were swinging loose from their hinges. He immediately assumed that all the prisoners had escaped, and he was about to kill himself, figuring that he was as good as dead anyway. But Paul stopped him, shouting: "Don't do that! We are all still here!" The guard was upset as he collapsed in front of Paul and Silas. As he led them out of the jail he asked "Sirs, what must I do to be saved?" Paul and Silas were beaten, put in jail for the sole purpose of telling this jailer about Jesus. Talk about an adverse situation but the outcome was awesome as the jailor and his family put their trust in God. They shouted out praises to God. He delivered them and they were set free!

Through it all can you and I praise our Lord for what He has brought us through? The pain of sexual abuse is grueling, shattering, and consumes our lives, but can we praise God for what He has done? He takes the broken places in our lives and heals us. He never condemns us even when we are angry and rebelling against his authority. The Master is searching for a vessel to use, one that is empty, broken, and helpless. He chooses to cleanse it and make it whole, a vessel filled with His power and glory. Then He speaks to that vessel He has cleansed. There's a work for you to do. Go in my power, pour out your love to my innocent children that have been abused, Use your knowledge and experience to glorify my name and set children and women free=.

Adversity does not have to define us. We can become overcomers and reach out to others that are hurting. Are you able to see any good in what happened to you? In some ways the abuse so impacted my life, I really didn't want to live, but I could have been aborted or totally destroyed mentally as many young children are. God still loved me even though I was broken and needed fixing.

Ponder on these two questions
1. How do you respond to adversity? List the negative and positive ways that you respond.
2. Are you allowing your past to control you?

THE PRICE OF INTIMACY

How do we define intimacy? Intimacy is defined as familiarity, closeness, a caring warm connection with someone. It is understanding and confidence in that relationship; and seeking the good for that individual. Intimacy is developed as the relationship grows. Just recently while being on a prayer line I heard that vulnerability is a pathway to intimacy. That is a powerful statement that we must be vulnerable to have an intimate relationship with anyone including God.

How do I know if I can handle a truly intimate relationship? How can I prepare for it? As a teenager the thought of being intimate with a man and enjoying it was so frightening. I had shut down all my feelings and lack of trust prevented me from becoming connected to anyone beyond a superficial relationship. Many of my friends talked about sex as if it was a great experience but I wanted nothing to do with sex itself. If I was to describe myself as a teenager I would probably say I was a tease. Sex was not an option for me although I liked all the things that led up to having sex.

I thought that after getting married, everything would be just fine. I married an older man who was gentle and kind but he wanted a healthy sex life. I believed that my past would not affect my marriage. I was very wrong. He was not abusive but certain things he did or said often caused flashbacks to the abuse. Those flashbacks triggered the same reactions I had when my father abused me, and I immediately shut down and did not respond. It was not his intent to hurt me but it was my inability to explain why certain things caused fear and confusion.

Eventually memories came to taunt me, especially during intimate times. Sometimes I ended up punishing him and myself because of the pain, fear, and agony of trying to deal with sexual demands. My husband became a part of my hurting past because I kept pushing him away. I thought if I just could hide my pain, things would be all right. The truth was that deception about the abuse caused us to have a very dysfunctional intimate life. It was easier to avoid sex than to attempt to deal with my emotions and reactions.

The price of becoming intimate in a man/woman relationship is usually very difficult for sexually abused women. I didn't speak of the sexual abuse to my husband until about three months before he passed away. Many women are never able to have a true intimate relationship with a man; they often resort to lesbian relationships, are frigid or become promiscuous because of their background. Survivors frequently have difficulties with trust, commitment, sex, and intimacy which have a direct impact on relationships.

The question is when do you tell the one you are in a relationship with about the fact you have been raped, and sexually abused or do you tell them? God doesn't want our relationships to just be surface relationships. He created us for physical and emotional intimacy with the opposite sex.

When I was a child and was being sexually abused, experiencing conflicting sensations such as pain, anger, humiliation, and even arousal, I shut down and often fantasized that these things were happening to another child. I became emotionally immune to the pain, and refused to cry. I often disassociated when I felt threatened or sexually aroused. As a survivor I needed to be in control all the time because I was afraid of rejection and losing control.

Intimacy was established quickly in my relationship with my husband, but as we got closer, barriers were erected. I needed more distance and found that intimacy was terrifying for me. I struggled with certain actions of my husband when he wanted sex. I could not tell him why I was afraid of letting go and having an orgasm. My unmet childhood needs created barriers as I strived to deal with actually being a partner instead of a victim in sexual intimacy. Intimacy needs a foundation of trust, vulnerability, and the ability to give as well as receive. To me intimacy was a matter of someone controlling what was going to happen to my body and I would shut down emotionally.

Do you hear the cry of my heart?
When I say, ""I'm fine"
Wounded, I hide
Denying my pain
Unable to confront
The terror of the night
Can you accept me if I really
Express the cry of my heart?
Or will you cast me aside
Or cause me great pain?
Can I trust you with my heart?
I really don't know.

We were created for intimacy with God and others. We need to be vulnerable enough to share and work on intimacy. Intimacy is a physical and spiritual oneness in any relationship. Likewise, God doesn't want our interaction with Him to end at salvation, that's just where it begins. Intimacy with God is a spiritual oneness and you must desire it with all your heart.

> Psalms 42:1-2 states "As the deer pants for streams of water. So my soul pants for you, God. My soul thirsts for God, for the living God. Where can I go and meet with God?" In times of trouble, affliction, or opposition we should turn to God as our ultimate refuge, helper, deliverer, and provider.

Psalms 42:1-2 describes a man's deep longing in his heart for an intimate relationship with God. Intimacy with God requires sacrifice and a deep longing to be in such close connection with God, we long to praise Him, to pray, and to be in His Word. With that being said, intimacy with God must mean that we take off our masks, surrender our past, and seek His face and will for our lives. Trust is a major factor in developing an intimate relationship with anyone, including God.

After accepting Jesus as my Lord, many blessings from God filled my life and God used me in various ministries. The problem was that I still hid behind my "Safe" masks and continued to reside in the city of bondage. I wanted to have victory over the past but I never seemed to accomplish that goal. I often spoke of becoming more like Mary, sitting at the feet of Jesus, worshiping and learning from Him, but I was too busy about all my activities. It was as if I had to prove to God that I was worthy of His love. One night at a revival meeting, the evangelist asked the congregation if they wanted something different from God.

As I went to the altar that night I asked for the evangelist to pray for me about having a more intimate walk with the Lord. The evangelist asked me three times if I was sure this was what I wanted before he prayed for me. In my own prideful way, I said, yes. He said he would pray for me but I needed to realize the pathway wasn't going to be easy. That was an understatement. I thought I knew what I was asking for but I didn't know the cost of intimacy would change my life. He said, holiness is a part of having an intimate walk with the Lord.

I was in a long lasting relationship that needed changing. Shortly after this a friend addressed this issue in my life also and asked me to be accountable to her. I had never been accountable to anyone about anything especially about something personal. She began to instruct me in the holiness walk with God through ministry tapes and books. Even though I respected her, wanted that intimate walk with the Lord, I didn't see the need to end my longstanding relationship with the man I had been dating for almost twenty years. I was sure we could still be good friends. It was over a year before my relationship came to an abrupt end, and even then it wasn't my choice but God's love intervened again in my life. Ending the relationship and moving to Georgia was difficult but I knew it was God's will. The first few months I was extremely depressed and still staying in contact with the man I had dated for twenty years. That tie had to be broken for me to begin to heal and move on with an intimate relationship with God. The first step to acquiring an intimate love relationship with God is to realize that the life He promises can never be found in another person. True intimacy with God is a bond between His heart and ours. It is a personal relationship where God loves me and I love Him. It's sitting at His feet and learning from Him. Just as a close relationship with another person requires conversation, so does our relationship with Jesus. He wants us to sit at His feet, seek His face, and commune with Him. He just wants us to tell Him what is on our heart.

Prayer is a two-way conversation, it's sharing and listening. It is vitally important that we are surrounded with other believers who have an intimate walk with the Lord. Remember that just as developing a relationship with a friend or significant other takes time, so it will be with Jesus. Open your heart to Jesus, the lover of your soul, and let Him fill you with His love.

God was calling me to a higher level of intimacy that required transparency. It was only as I studied and listened to the teaching my friend gave me, and became accountable to her that I realized God loved me enough to bring someone into my life to instruct me on holy living. It was her unconditional love that caused me to step out in faith and respond to God's call. God desires to make use of our less than perfect circumstances. He takes our vulnerability to open up about our past to bring hope and healing to others.

God's grace was more than sufficient for me. The recovery from sexual abuse, drug addiction, bulimia, and other addictive behaviors has been a process as I have surrendered my life more and more to God.

Healing is almost always a process. It begins with us realizing we have a wound that needs healing. We can put on a band aid or wear one of our many masks but unless we let it heal we are interfering with the process. One of my favorite words in the New Testament that refers to healing is immediately. Immediately they are healed, received their sight, and walked. Immediately the woman with the issue of blood was healed when she touched the hem of Jesus' garment. I like to call this microwave healing but we all know that even if the microwave heats things up quickly it does not stay hot very long. God wanted more for me. He wanted me to see that He was in control, and He was the deliverer.

Every time I prayed about the immediate healing of the sexual abuse, and delivery from the drug Xanax, God said He wanted to maximize my time with Him for the deliverance from the sexual abuse and drugs, that there were things I needed to learn and walk in before the healing would be complete. Either way God is our healer. But I must admit I would have preferred the microwave way!

God wanted me to have that intimate walk with Him. Spending time in prayer, the word of God, and beginning to praise God drew me into a closer walk with the Lord. When we realize we can't do it without Him we begin to develop that relationship of dependence and intimacy with Him. He is El Roi, "The God who sees me." He sees the brokenness controlling my life and declares that I am precious in His sight, forgiven, and loved. Until you are broken, you don't know what you are made of. It gives you the ability to build yourself all over again, but you will be stronger than before.

If God can take a pile of old dry bones, cause them to rise up into a mighty army, He surely can take the broken pieces of our lives and transform us into mighty warriors, bringing us to a place of intimacy with Him. The question is do you want to get well, and have victory over all the addictive behaviors you have developed.

Jesus calls us friends. True friendship is rare on earth. It means identifying with someone in thought, heart, and spirit. The whole experience of life is to enable us to enter into a close relationship with Jesus. We receive His blessings and know His Word, but do we really know Him? The bearing of fruit is always shown in Scripture to be the visible result of an intimate relationship with Jesus. The outcome of intimacy with Jesus is a life of surrender. Jesus is in fact the model of intimacy with God because He and the Father are one. No relationship can be closer than that oneness with the Father that Jesus experienced. If we hope to obtain that type of intimacy with God, Jesus must be our model.

Intimacy requires a sacrifice, a sacrifice of our self-will even as Jesus modeled for us in the Garden of Gethsemane when He said, "Not my will, but thine be done."

Thoughts to mediate upon:
1. Are you willing to die to self and let God reign?
2. What do you conceive as the price of intimacy for you?
3. If you have been sexually abused, how does it affect your relationships with others?
4. If you are married or planning on getting married, will you tell your significant other about your past?
5. What do you consider as a normal relationship?

BROKEN AND CAST ASIDE

Broken and cast aside, I felt unloved and used. What do I dare talk about? Can I speak of the ugliness of sexual abuse? Dare I tell you the times I tried to stab my father with a knife in the middle of the night? Can I tell you how dirty he made me feel when he demanded that I performed oral sex on him? Can I tell you how I would sneak downstairs, brush my teeth again and again, throw up and still feel dirty? Can I tell you of the times I hid in the corn fields, running aimlessly away from my father? Or should I tell you of the times I wished I still had a daddy I could run to who would pick me up and swing me around telling me he loved me? I was daddy's little girl until I was five years old.

But now I am so broken. It seemed like part of me was crumbled into tiny little pieces like a hard clod of dirt when you step on it. I wished somebody would look beyond the barriers I had established and see the little girl who cried herself to sleep at night only to be awakened to perform sexual acts that made her hurt. I wanted to be loved, not used as a throw-away toy after someone else had pleasured themselves. Where was the God my Sunday school teacher had talked about, the God that was a good father?

I remember a time when I dropped one of my mothers' salt and pepper shakers and it broke in many pieces. I tried to put them back together with glue but it didn't work. How do you glue love back together again when you have been sexually or emotionally abused? For many years I thought of my heart as being broken into many pieces. There was just a little small chamber of my heart that still longed for my daddy to love me. Another chamber was filled with terrifying memories, destructive dreams, and fear. I often sat and drew pictures of my heart with jagged edges, with tears and blood dropping out of it into the dirt, never to be healed again. Is your past keeping you broken and feeling unloved as mine has for many years?

Brokenness has many faces and mine is one of them; a face that is cracked, a crooked smile, eyes that are shadowed with fear and distrust. It was a face that was bleeding, hiding from the truth that my daddy really didn't love me. His love was broken by sin and abuse. I wish I knew why and what had changed my daddy. For years it seemed like my broken crushed heart was beyond repair, couldn't ever know what real love was meant to be. I cowered in shame, fleeing from the darkest memories and the pain, running away from anyone who said they loved me. Is it too much to ask God if this broken cracked heart of mine could once again experienced real love?

Brokenness is defined as being forcibly separated into two or more pieces, damaged, and many times damaged beyond repair. It is defined spiritually as the shattering of one's soul. You recognize brokenness because you can feel it. When facing our personal brokenness, any hope of restoration often eludes us, and we feel that it is safer to accept the loss of our safety, virginity, and real family relationships rather than address the issues of sexual abuse.

But God uses our brokenness to break the cycle of shame and guilt. He delivers us from our enemies and heals us from within. "The Lord is close to the broken-hearted, He rescues those crushed in spirit." Psalms 14:18 Shout it out. God loves you! He delivers and set you free to worship Him.

Often God uses our brokenness to deal with our self-reliance. Most sexually abused children become control freaks when they grow up. Everything has to be done a certain way at a certain time, and please don't interrupt our pattern. Brokenness is not punishment. The apostle Paul had a thorn in his flesh which kept him from exalting himself. We each have our own brokenness that we need to address. Each day, Jesus invites us to ask for His help to repair whatever is broken in our lives. We don't have to wait until we have a long list of problems. We can come to Him anytime with full assurance, knowing He is available to heal our brokenness right now. No appointment is needed. He just wants to love us right where we are. You can never be so broken that God can't put the pieces back together.

I have heard stories about abuse that would rock your world; women raped, sold into prostitution, and beaten until they ended up in the emergency room. But what about the little children who cannot tell their story? I have spoken to many young women who have turned to drugs, alcohol, or prostitution because they felt worthless, just an object to be used for sexual depravity by some man. There are many women who are married, unable to have normal sexual relationships with their spouse because of continued sexual abuse as a child. Sexual abuse destroys normal sexual relationships not addressed timely. My heart is broken when I hear about sexual abuse by leaders in churches. Some women I have spoken to never recover from this abuse and never will trust God. Does God's heart hurt when his leaders abuse children?

Jean Anouilh says:
"Our entire life consists ultimately in accepting ourselves as we are."

One of the greatest tragedies is to lose your own sense of self by hiding behind a mask. The masks I wore for many years were to hide the pain, the fear, and anger that consumed me. Each day I put on my mask to hide the pain, yet I wished that someone, anyone, would look closely enough to see how sad I really was. I often asked myself will the real me please stand up; but fear kept me immobilized. I could not heal myself. I chose the path of least resistance and I thought the least amount of pain. Pain hidden by drugs, alcohol, or other methods of denial does not heal itself.

The walls I had intentionally built around myself needed to crumble, but I had to take that first step of obedience toward Jesus. I was consumed by a deep pit of pain, suffering, and despair. Often I felt totally helpless and it seemed like desperation surrounded me from every side. Many times I simply did not care nor did I know how to escape till one day a friend told me about Jesus.

I will not even pretend to know how dark or how deep your suffering has been. But may I suggest that just maybe God works from seemingly hopeless situations to bring us into His loving care? I took my broken dreams to God, but instead of leaving them at the altar; I picked them up again. My dreams were gone, my life was a mess. I could not put my broken life back together. But God could when I submitted it all to Him.

I'm sure you all know the story of Humpty Dumpty. A friend of mine gave me a stuffed Humpty Dumpty pillow but never finished sewing it together because neither she nor I thought I could put my life back together. Humpty Dumpty was an egg, a symbol of fertility but also vulnerable, and as we all know eggs are easily broken. Humpty was sitting on a wall, maybe just enjoying the view from up there. A wall separates two areas, but it can also separate two courses of action. The fence in this wall symbolizes to me the valley of indecision. To me this meant that I was too afraid to really commit to find my true purpose here on earth, to find healing, and live the life that God wanted me to live. I came to this conclusion because the next line in this book speaks that Humpty Dumpty had a great fall. All the king's men could not put Humpty Dumpty back together again. All the books I read, all the counseling and conferences I went to, all the drugs I depended upon could not put me back together again. Only the King of Kings could take the broken pieces of my life and begin the process of healing and restoration.

For years my walls were too high, too dangerous, and too emotional for me to attempt to receive healing in my life. Sitting on the wall of indecision, giving into all of the fears that haunted my life, stopped my progress towards healing. Yet God wanted to penetrate the darkest places of my heart. We simply can't grow and be healed without including the joy and pain, the love and hate, the fear and anger, and learning to walk in forgiveness.

Because of our brokenness, God can do great things through us. When we look in the mirror we can see God working through us as He heals the broken pieces and restores us to victory. All I could see in the mirror was a reflection of a young troubled women without any hope. I needed to believe that someone loved me.

Falling is built into our destiny just like Humpty's when we have been cast aside. We actually need to become vulnerable and realize that God can help us. Our defenses and walls that we have erected must be broken into thousands of pieces to receive healing. Human knowledge will fail to reconstruct our life without God being involved. If you find yourself in the valley of indecision, too afraid to move forward and face the darkness of your past, perhaps you can take the risk of applying God's grace to the darkness of your spirit. God's grace is sufficient for the task of healing us from sexual abuse.

Will God's grace run out if we keep running from the truth? Are you surrounded by pain that seems too deep for you to express? Getting over a painful past is like flying a kite. Sometimes we get caught up in the trees, the lies we have been told, the masks we have worn for years, believing that nothing can change or heal our brokenness. We walk in denial, deep depression, and close ourselves off from those who can help us.

One day I realized God could pull me out of the deepest pits of depression, take His eraser to the whiteboard and wipe away the shame and pain. It was then that I could accept that the concept of radical obedience to God would heal all of my wounds, not some but all of them. He redeemed my pain that I might share with others His healing power.

God created us to be naked and unashamed. Fig leaves and masks were man's idea because of sin. Sin creates barriers that God never intended to happen. Shame keeps us from speaking out. Fear establishes a root inside of us that keeps us tangled in lies and deception. I didn't think I could speak or write about my story of sexual abuse. What would people think of me?

Remember the women at the well. She went from hiding her brokenness to proclaiming come and see the man who forgave all my sins. He gave her living water. He knew her story but yet he told her go and call her husband and come back. She replied I have no husband. Jesus said to her, "You are right when you say you have no husband. The fact is you have had five husbands, and the man you now have is not your husband." Jesus knows all about our past, the sins that have been committed against us and the sins we have committed, and still forgives and loves us.

In order to minister to other women with our story of redemption we must relinquish pride, remove our masks, and become genuine. The truth speaks volumes to the hearts of children, men and women who have been abused. The need of revealing the truth about our brokenness and our shattered dreams is the starting place for changing lives, mine, yours and others. When we humble ourselves and become servants of God we have nothing to lose. Redemption and healing will come to many women and children as we reveal the truth of God's love and forgiveness. Can you see yourself as God sees you, precious in His sight and loved unconditionally? God sees our value even when we can't see past the brokenness in our lives.

Romans 8:31-33

If God be for us, who can be against us? He who did not spare His own son, but gave him up for us all, how will he not also, along with Him, graciously give us all things? Who will bring any charge against those whom God has chosen? It is God who justifies.

Can we take our crushed, bleeding hearts; our lives who never knew what love was meant to be and lay them at the foot of the cross? Can we flee from the darkest memories, from the deepest shame, and lay our wounded hearts and broken lives at the Lord's feet? Will God take the broken pieces and heal us?

Psalms 61:1-3 reads as follows: "Hear my cry, O' Lord, listen to my prayer. From the ends of the earth I call to you. I call as my heart grows faint. Lead me to the rock that is higher than I, for you have been my refuge, a strong tower against the foe."

Does God say that He is the God who makes a way in the wilderness and will never forsake us? He was always there waiting for me to run to Him. I didn't know His love was unconditional, that He paid the price. I took my wounded bleeding heart which never knew what love was meant to be, and asked the Lord to heal the wounds. My prayer to God was open my eyes, heal my broken heart and make me whole. God never throws broken people away. He takes our brokenness, wraps us in His love, and restores us to wholeness. His love delivers and sets free!

Think upon the following questions.
1. Are you feeling broken, unable to find restoration?
2. Have you made an attempt to seek help?
3. Have you told anyone your story or reached out to a counselor?
4. Will the real you stand up and claim victory?

REAL LOVE WALKS THROUGH THE PAIN TO REDEEM YOU

Adolf Quezada in the book "Loving yourself for God's Sake" makes the following statement. "Love yourself without any conditions. Love yourself through the defensiveness and the darkness of your past. Love yourself beyond whatever you deserve for such is the love of God."

This is a powerful statement for children and women who have been sexually or physically abused. Many sexually abused children including myself have a difficult time of loving ourselves and others. When I discovered the truth about how valuable God's children are, I decided I would try to walk in what God thinks about me. As one of my friends repeatedly says I am a princess because God loves me unconditionally. I am special, unique, and one of God's kids. I am God's masterpiece, unique down to my fingerprints. Because of that security, I am finding self-worth and value in Christ. Like a lump of clay in the Masters hands I am being molded by life's experiences into a perfect vessel of service for Jesus.

I could chose the strongholds I had built all around myself or I could choose to become a part of God's plan for my life. The strongholds were like a cancer, eating away at my deepest desire for intimacy with the Lord. Holding close the veil of self-protection, I longed to reach out to experience the love of God. But my image of God was more like the image of an angry father who could never accept me; one who had been defiled, raped and trapped with a mask on all the time. The problem of the sin of sexual abuse is that it is always with us, silently accusing us that we are worthless, damaged goods.

I felt hopelessly unfit for God to consider me. I struggled with the thought that God could never forgive me. Why would God want a child or woman that was totally rebellious, stubborn and filled with hatred? It seemed like because of what had happened to me and other sexually abused children that God really didn't care. God keeps pouring His love into our hearts. Unfortunately, the image that God has of us when He calls us His daughters or sons bears virtually no resemblance to our own self-image. God is love! I felt totally unlovable and found it difficult to believe anyone could love me. But God's love delivers and set us free.

True freedom starts when we break free from the enemy's lies and completely surrender to God. Shame causes us to hide. Take a look at Adam and Eve. They were naked and until they sinned; they walked with God in the garden and were not ashamed. After they sinned they took fig leaves and made clothes for themselves. Shame causes fear and we put on our masks, afraid to tell what has happened to us. An abused child is always told to never tell. That secret covers the sin of the abuse and causes the victim to walk in fear and the abuser to continue with his or her heinous acts of depravity. All the while the abuser professes his or her love for you. And you and I, continue to believe love hurts and destroys.

It's time to break the power of silence. Being real is what really matters, no pretending, no masks, no trying to always leave a good impression. In spite of our imperfections, we have been chosen by God for a task that perfectly fits our talents. He will not throw you into the trash like a broken toy. Pain, struggles, and adversity may be a part of our lives. But regardless of our circumstances or sins God takes the broken pieces of our lives, interrupts us with His marvelous love, restores us, and uses our struggles to glorify His name.

If you are wrapping yourself up to conceal any vulnerability, whatever happens to you has to go through the many masks you are wearing. Because of this, the one thing you are searching for, love,-doesn't ever reach where you truly are. Who hasn't had the experience of asking someone whether anything is wrong, only to hear the words, "I'm fine." Strong people wearing masks don't let themselves cry, right? We just wonder if we have the strength to survive another crushing blow to our already bleeding heart.

Jesus knew the feeling of His heart being crushed. In Mark 14:34 it is written "My soul is overwhelmed with sorrow to the point of death." Jesus was facing a cruel death, death on the cross. He was beaten, a crown of thorns placed upon His head, mocked and nailed to a cross. He did this for us. But crushing is not the end, not for Jesus and not for us. Jesus died but He rose from the dead as He had promised. We too can have the victory. It is time to shout it out that God delivers and sets us free.

Most of us are concerned that revealing our pain might lead to others treating us differently or reacting negatively to our story. I experienced a negative reaction from a very close friend and almost gave up the fight to be an overcomer when my book "Broken Chains" was released. For a few months I was so depressed I just didn't want to go on. I relied on prescription drugs to cope with the normal daily activities until I was totally addicted to the drugs. It was almost like walking around in a coma, unable to cope with the pain of betrayal.

When we have an unpleasant past, we find ourselves trying to convince others that we are acceptable. If we can only reveal our pain, our vulnerability becomes compassion and empathy and the world could use more of that.

God then equips us for the purpose He has ordained for our lives. No matter what trials, illness, or heartaches we have endured, our lives still matter to God. Now I can look in the mirror and see how precious God thinks I am. I am His beloved daughter, redeemed from my past. You may feel like I have, trapped in darkness, depression, and unable to see the glory of God, His protection, and His plan for your life.

The very act of praise releases the power of God into a set of circumstances that you think are immoveable, and enables God to change them. Encountering God today can transform your life. I want to passionately pursue the one who loves me more than anyone, Jesus, my redeemer and healer. I want to be become known as a woman of praise and thanksgiving because God's love turned my world upside down. We can face every storm with confidence as long as we hold to God's unchanging hand.

Walk with me today, face every storm in your life, and experience victory. God makes the first move as he awakens in you a hunger and thirst for victory. In Joshua 24:15 we see that Joshua made a decision. "Choose for yourselves this day whom you will serve, but as for me and my house, we will serve the Lord." Whom are you going to serve, the Lord or are you going to remain stuck in your past? We can continue to dwell in the past, be attached to our memories, and never progress toward healing; or we can allow God to do something new and miraculous in our life. After all, He is God and makes a way in the wilderness and streams in the wasteland. His love is real and never ending.

My past was anything but typical, but I am sure there are many who have had experiences that would cause most people to shudder if their stories could be heard. I have heard stories that rock my world- women who have been raped, sexually abused, sold into prostitution, and beaten until they ended up in the emergency room. I have seen and spoken to women who have turned to drugs, alcohol, and prostitution because they felt worthless; just an object to be used by some man. I have talked to women who married and were unable to have normal sexual relationships. Sexual abuse destroys normal relationships if not addressed timely.

For fifty years I chose the path of least resistance and I thought the least amount of pain. One day I took my broken dreams to God, but then instead of leaving them at the altar, I picked them up again, thinking I could fix my broken life. My dreams were gone, my life was a mess. Still I thought I could pick up the pieces and put my life back together. After all, who knew the story and pain better than I did?

GOD DID!

My heart was bleeding and crushed, I never knew what love was meant to be. I hungered for the touch of love but retreated from the touch of any who said they loved me. I struggled to taste of what love and life could be like if only my wounded heart could trust in love once again. As a young child my heart's desire was for someone to just love me. I often asked the question what is wrong with me that nobody loves me. When you are accepted just the way you are and realize that someone loves you, it restores your self-worth, and gives you a purpose Love empowers you to follow your dreams. Love forgives the abuser. Shout it out loud and clear. God's unconditional love delivers and sets you free.

Our sexuality is at the very core of our identity. One of the most dramatic and overwhelming facts about child molestation and rape is the awakening of sexual desires at an age when the child does not even understand what is happening in their bodies.

My father molested me and eventually raped me. It was our secret. I wasn't supposed to tell anyone what happened. Daddy said he loved me and it wouldn't always hurt. The sexual molestation continued for many years until one day he raped me. Again it was my secret; how could I tell anyone the ugly truth of what was happening? How could I tell anyone that it wasn't just my father but he taught his two oldest sons it was okay to abuse children and women? My mother did not believe me, so why would anyone else believe me. From that day forward I was completely changed. I was scared, traumatized, and walked in fear never knowing what each day would bring.

The little girl who laughed and played was gone. She only wanted to hide from her daddy and mommy. Where could I go to hide? No-one believed me; not even my mother. I was locked in a dark closet for many hours when I resisted my father. Fear of the darkness became my enemy. It has only been recently that I have been able to sleep in a dark house. We can chose to dwell in the past, hide from the pain, or allow God to do something new and miraculous in our life.

I remember screaming, "Where was God when I needed Him?" But today I asked myself where was I when Jesus cried out in a loud voice, "My God, my God, why have you forsaken me?" Mark 15:34

Does not God say, He's the God who makes a way in the wilderness and streams in the wasteland and will never forsake us? He was always there waiting for me to run to Him. I didn't know His love was unconditional. Not until someone stepped into my life; and said it didn't matter what I had done, or what was done to me, God still loved me and forgave me. My prayer to God was open my eyes that I might see that the unnatural love I experienced from my abusers was never meant to be.

After years of pretending my emotional scars didn't exist and wearing many masks to conceal them from others, my hearts' cry was hear my prayer God and heal my heart.

Many of us are like a broken toy that can't be fixed. At one time we've been hurt, betrayed, left out, and abused. We've been conditioned to put on a smile and pretend we aren't broken. The problem is that broken things don't fix themselves. We put on our mask and simply exist. We can't trust people who are supposed to love and protect us. We seek attention and affection and realize that it is almost always followed by sexual demands. We don't have control over our body; other people's needs come ahead of our own needs.

Sadly many people are emotionally limping through life, pretending they are okay, instead of seeking healing from God who can give it. They ignore the pain, develop many stress related habits to control or hide the pain. Many become addicted to drugs, alcohol, and perverse sexual behaviors even to the extent of becoming abusers themselves. But the pain never heals; it just keeps exploding in various destructive behaviors.

We may attend support group meetings, seek extensive counseling, attend conferences, and still never receive complete healing. Only God can erase the past, take away the shame and guilt and mend our brokenness. Only God can make us whole. While we may never be as good as new, it may not be easy, and it will probably take time, God can certainly mend our brokenness.

Psalms 61: 1-3
Hear my cry, God; listen to my prayer, from the ends of the earth I will call to you. I call as my heart grows faint. Lead me to the rock that is higher than I. For you have been my refuge a strong tower against the foe.

Think on these things:
1. Do you still allow your past to dominate your future?
2. How have you coped with situations beyond your control?
3. Have you sought counseling or been able to talk to a friend?
4. I challenge you to write your thoughts down and contemplate on them.
5. Revisit the past one step at a time, letting God love you through the abuse.

WE CAN'T GIVE AWAY SOMETHING
WE DON'T HAVE

Today I was asked seven questions about love. I added one more question. What does love look like? My first response was I really don't know, and then I thought of I Corinthians, Chapter 13. If our love or being loved is based on this chapter we would always feel cherished. Without love I am nothing. Love is not self-seeking, it does not delight in evil, neither is it self-seeking. It protect, always trusts and never fails. Love does not punish and is not based on your performance.

But as a child who was told that daddy loved her, and given gifts when she was cooperative, my concept of love was based on my performance and dispensable after I was abused. Giving or receiving love is difficult when it is based on your performance while being sexually abused. Love is the greatest thing in the world, so how do we explain sexual abuse by a father or mother. I ask myself did either one of my parents know what love was or how to love their children? I really do not know what happened in their lives that caused them to be sexually, emotionally, and physically abusive.

I really did believe my daddy loved me until someone told me about my heavenly Father. There was no comparison. My little girl heart tried to heal itself by developing an inner strength. Only that strength build a wall, instead of a bridge, to God's heart. My independence kept me from a deeper relationship with God. I learned to act like I loved God, but really didn't trust Him with my heart or problems. My concept of God's love was based on the fact I was not worthy. I deserved to be punished. If the Lord loved me would He have allowed so much abuse, so much pain?

God's love does not have to be earned. It just is unconditional love. I have a reindeer sitting on my bookcase that a dear friend gave to me. On its foot are the words Jesus loves me. When my heart is overwhelmed and filled with sorrow I begin to realize that I never had real love from my parents but Jesus loves me just as I am. He doesn't expect me to perform in any certain way to earn his love, he just loves me as I am. God has blessed me with friends that love me with all my little quirks and encourage me to be all that Jesus wants me to be.

My heart was closed, broken, and not willing to admit that I wasn't fine. I did need help but in a way that my self-sufficiency simply couldn't provide. As an adult I had to learn what it meant to have a daddy God who loved me perfectly. Sometimes the pain from what didn't happen was as real as the pain from the abuse. I saw myself as flawed, a cracked pot, and wondered how anyone can love me.

1. Have you ever been in love?
2. What does love mean to you?
3. What does love look like?
4. How did it benefit your life?
5. How do you know someone loves you?
6. How does it make you feel?
7. What does it feel like when you love yourself?
8. Who do you love and for what reason?

Most of us would probably answer the first question, have you ever been in love with one word, yes. But if we don't understand what love really is, is it love or lust that we are partaking of? Love can be defined as a feeling, a passion for, a devotion to, a friendship, worship of or tenderness for a person or object. Lust is defined as a hunger, or very strong sexual desire. Lust has its focus on pleasing oneself, and it leads to unwholesome actions to fill our desires with no regard to the consequences of another person. Lust is about possession. Sexual abuse is always about possession. It does not benefit the recipient.

Receiving love can be very difficult when we don't know what it means. Walking in love does not come easily to those who have been abused. Each time we choose to love someone, it will cost us something-time, money, or effort. We were created to live a life filled with love, but became broken when we were abused.

What does love mean to you? Is it just a feeling or is it so much more? How do you love without being trapped or used by the other person? My whole concept of love was distorted when I was a child. Daddy said he loved me when I performed or did not resist when he molested me; but my heart was broken because love really hurt. Maybe he did love me in his own way; but something was broken in our relationship that left me desperate for reassurance. Many of my boy friends said they loved me until I refused to have sex with them, then they dumped me and chose a girl who would perform. If this was all there was to love was it worth it to be in a relationship? My mother never told me she loved me until she was on her death bed. It was so difficult to respond to love at that time. I am so sorry I never told her that I loved her but the pain was so great that I just couldn't say the words. But God's love interrupted my life again as he spoke to my heart in the nursing home that day. It was as if he spoke the words out loud, lightning struck and thunder roared as he said to me "I brought her back to let her tell you that she loved you. That is how much I love you."

What is love? What does love look like? How do you love with both compassion and honesty? On that day in the nursing home God showed me what love really was. I had always wanted my mother to say she loved me but when she said she did I responded with anger. God spoke to my heart in that nursing home that He loved me so much He was the one who granted this desire of my heart. That was love beyond anything I could have ever imagined.

What does love mean to you if you have a failing marriage, an abortion, or a sexually abusive relationship as a child or an abusive relationship as an adult? Were you really in love with your husband in the beginning or after you got pregnant and had to get married? Many women are in physically and verbally abusive relationships and still declare they love the person they are with. Love in these cases many times is simply that they are afraid to be alone, or in many cases so accustomed to being abused that they accept any form of attention.

How does love benefit you if you go into a relationship without being totally honest? I never told my husband I had been repeatedly sexually abused until we were married almost ten years. Is love just a feeling or is it an action? Does your love for someone cause you to be open, vulnerable, and to trust? I know that I loved my husband but truthfully by not sharing that I was sexually abused created problems in our relationship. I thought if I could just be what he wanted in a wife, everything would be fine. But on the day my husband passed away, the one thing that he said he wanted in marriage I didn't give to him. He wanted a wife that loved the Lord.

Today, I ask myself how marital love benefited my life. I experienced that love was so much more than sex. It was giving back to another person, caring for them in the midst of illness, just reaching out and holding each other without being expected to perform some sexual act. The constant affirmations of how good a wife I was made me feel cherished and want to share special moments of love with my husband. It is so basic to want to feel loved, cherished, and cared for. In the midst of the trials I found it was possible to work through disagreements without expectations of having to perform some sexual act.

Love created within me a desire to give forgiveness and have patience when it seemed like the world was falling apart. Love is intimacy that has nothing to do with sex. Love is being comfortable to share your most private thoughts with another person. Love is most often based on deep friendship that makes life suddenly seem complete. It is a mutual desire to be happy together and forever friends. Love gives, receives, endures, supports and makes life suddenly seem complete. Love is compassionate and brings hope in a desperate situation.

The secret to loving is dependence upon God for God is love. When we say yes to God and no to self our love becomes pure and then love brings light into darkness.

Being abused for many years as a child, the question how do you know if someone loves you is difficult to answer. We are conditioned to believe our performance is love. God is asking us to take a risk, let our guard down and love others as He loves us. It touches my heart to see an older couple still holding hands, and looking at each other with love.

Love takes time to share special moments, give special gifts, and just to be there for you when your heart is breaking. Love is a commitment until death do we part; it is communication that doesn't even take words, just a special caress or look. Love keeps its promises. Love is asking and caring, going the extra mile. Love is not about changing someone else; it requires compromise. Where can I find the energy to love when it feels like I am broken inside? I don't want to pretend that I love you; I want to take off the mask and be real.

How does love make you feel? Love makes me feel cherished, valuable and gives me the courage to reach out to others. To be loved unconditionally gives me the freedom to love again. Love moves past the physical to a spiritual level when love becomes unconditional. Unconditional love gives us the privilege to share on a deeper level of intimacy, gently corrects wrong assumptions, and causes us to grow spiritually. Love makes us feel good about ourselves.

What does it feel like when you love yourself?

According to Joel Osteen, You are not to criticize yourself. He instructs us not to go around all day thinking we are unattractive, or not smart. God wasn't having a bad day when He made you. If you don't love yourself in the right way you can't love your neighbor as you are supposed to do.

You need to be who God created you to be. In order to love yourself, you have to be real. Take off the mask and figure out what you really want. Loving takes time whether we are talking about loving ourselves or loving others. Learn to accept progress at any pace. We all need fresh beginnings and that means letting go of the past and its pain. Acknowledge your feelings. Cherish what you have learned from your challenges. To love as God instructs us to do we have to forgive ourselves and others. Learn from your challenges, celebrate your accomplishments. Stop saying bad things about yourself and embrace change and positive thinking.

Who do you love and for what reason?

At this point in my life I have experienced love from a friend that has changed my life. At one point in our relationship she said I will love you unconditionally no matter what you do. I not only felt her unconditional love but her family expressed that same kind of caring and love for me. Because of this I know love does not always hurt or cause destruction in our lives. I have realized that love will cause you to grow, will correct your behavior in a kind and instructive manner, and does not seek to destroy or cause you pain. Love does not betray you but lifts you up.

Do we only love those who only love us? If that is true we are falling very short of what God expects of us. We are to love our neighbor as ourselves and we are to love those who seek to destroy us.

God loves us unconditionally. We are precious in His sight. Is God enough or do we long for that kind of love that reaches out and touches us with warmth and support? God does! He sacrificed His only son, Jesus, because of his love for all mankind. God is love in the purest form.

Because sexual abuse affects emotional development, and we seek control, relationships are difficult for us. Unfortunately, many people are emotionally limping through life, pretending they are okay. Instead of seeking healing from God who can give it, they ignore the pain, or become involved with drugs or alcohol to the extent they are addicted. But the pain never heals-it just keeps popping up. Only God can make us whole. While we may never be good as new, it may not be easy, and it will probably take time, God can certainly mend our brokenness.

It is God's unconditional interruption of love that caused me to respond to His call and step out in faith. The guilt, the shame, the pain of my past does not disqualify me from moving on, to serve God, to be forgiven, and to have peace. However ugly or painful my scars are, they can be redeemed and even used by God. God doesn't want me to ignore the scar tissue in my heart, nor does He want me to run and hide. God desires to make use of our less than perfect circumstances. He takes our willingness to open up about our past and become real to bring hope and healing to others. God's grace was more than sufficient for me. What about you? When you examine your emotional heart, what do you see? Being fully me, open to others, sharing my pain is so much better than being an imitation of someone else. We are unique and God wants us to be real.

Through much prayer and wanting a more intimate walk with God I have been changed. The abuse is no longer the center of my life, and what a relief that is! It is a process not a five minute microwaved experience. I have a purpose to fulfil, a plan that God ordained me to complete, and I am no longer bound to hide the truth. We can be set free from sexual abuse, rape, addictions, promiscuity and eating disorders.

The Message Bible in James 1:2-4 states the following: "You know that your faith-life is forced into the open and shows its true colors. So don't try to get out of anything prematurely. Let it do its work so you become mature and well- developed, not deficient in any way."

73

Oliver Wendell Holmes must have understood about trials and tribulations when he wrote "If I had a formula for ridding mankind of trouble, I think I would not reveal it, for in doing so, I would do him a disservice."

Minimizing the abuse and its impact is tempting, but it doesn't help. The first step we must make is to acknowledge what happened and how it affected us. Unable to get past the pain and destruction in my life I found myself involved in many situations, self-denial, sexual abuse, bulimia, drug addictions, to name a few of the situations that kept me bound to the past for many years. All of these things have made me feel worthless, but God says I am precious to Him. He is El Roi, "The God who sees me."

He sees the broken woman, me, who felt so alone, unloved, and violated. He declares that I am precious in His sight, forgiven, and perfect. God loves you so much! He wants to restore the broken pieces and give you a new heart that is tender and obedient to Him. But you must choose to let go of the broken pieces and let God restore your life to wholeness. Will you come to Him for healing?

What amazing grace, that Jesus died for me, God's redemption at Christ's expense- Praise God! I am free to be me and to have victory! The truth is there is nothing we can do to earn God's love and forgiveness. It's not about us. It's only when we realize our powerlessness and accept ownership of what happened to us, that God will change the circumstances and make our scars beautiful. That means we must take off our masks and become real. We must confront the fear head on and know that God will be our confidence and that all things work together for the good of those who love and serve God. Cast your cares on the Lord and he will sustain you, he will never let the righteous fall. Psalms 55:22

God has captured my heart. What about you?

Today I embrace my femininity, the woman that God made, beauty that God has restored. Yes, I embrace intimacy with my Creator, my bridegroom. Peace and joy flood my heart because I am loved. I am His child. He calls me His beloved, His bride to be. I have come to sit at His feet, my deliverer and protector. His presence is so near as He pursues my heart, and I am secure in His love. He gives me a shield of victory, his hand sustains me when I am weak. His mercies are new every morning. His love upholds me when I falter and when I fear what man can do. He protects me from trouble and surrounds me with beautiful songs of deliverance.

Psalms 22:8

He who trusts in the Lord, let the Lord rescue him, let Him deliver him, since he delights in him

Consider these question and write your thoughts out.

1. How do you define love?
2. Do you struggle with loving yourself?
3. Do you see God as a loving Father?
4. How do you practice receiving and giving love?
5. Will you take time to consider these questions and God's purpose for your life?

THE FEAR FACTOR OF SEXUAL ABUSE

W alk with me as we look at fear and how it affects our recovery. For many staying in a prison is more comfortable than taking off the masks and dealing with the issues of the abuse. A life of bondage seems easier for us for we do not have to face our shame, pain, and fears. But is it really easier? Is it safer, or even beneficial for your physical, emotional, sexual, or spiritual health? Do you fear that your mask will slip off one day? Do you live in terror of unexpected exposure of your fear and pain? The mask must stay in place! If it comes off I feel that I won't survive. Sometimes I fear that it will fall off before I am ready to deal with the pain, and then I will never quit crying.

Think back how fear and bitterness denies us freedom from our past. I hated my fears and struggled with my insecurities. I wondered if I would ever get past the fear of the dark and the fear of being locked in dark places. There were nights that I would hear my father come stumbling in the house. I knew he would be looking for me but there wasn't anywhere to hide. What's wrong with me that I cower in fear unable to speak of the atrocities that plagued my life? Is it my fault as my mother claimed? Why do I keep hiding behind a mask of fear unable to face the darkness of night? It seems as if I am paralyzed and cannot move from the pain of the past. I hate that each night my father came home stumbling I knew I had to try to hide but there never was a safe place that he didn't find me. His threats to me about abusing my sisters often times made me want to kill him.

The sides of my self-imposed prison are slippery with anger, betrayal, fear, and self-pity. There is only a tiny exit through the passage to freedom. Step in with me and see the prisoners. They are victims of betrayal, abuse, fear, and anger. You and I, like many can choose to chain ourselves to the past. But remember you are the one that suffers, not the abuser. In the comic strip "Peanuts" Linus gives Charlie Brown some advice. "I don't like to face problems head on. I think the best way to solve problems is to avoid them. He continues to say, "There is no problem so big or complicated that you can't run away from it."

Fear just keeps escalating if you refuse to face it head on. Physical and sexual abuse brings terror into the life of a child. Anger was usually present but fear kept me from expressing it. Fear was my worst enemy as I was always on guard and couldn't express joy or anger over anything. Trusting anyone was too dangerous. Fear dominated my life, the decisions I made, and the way I responded to others long after childhood.

I like to define fear as false evidence appearing real. Imagine a world that is full of fear; you cannot go anywhere without wondering who is going to attack you, and the darkness terrifies you. Do not hide from your fear or pretend it's not there. Fearfulness is a form of bondage and trust is the door of freedom. Cast all your anxieties on Jesus, for He will deliver you. If we are serving God with our whole heart we have nothing to fear.

I cannot say that overcoming fear has been easy for me. For years I would not sleep in a house without a light on, even though the danger of being sexually abused had stopped. Fear controlled my thoughts if I got locked in an apartment, elevator, or building with no means of escape. I am now dealing with a form of Fraud ID and the fear seems to be controlling my thoughts daily, in my home and wherever I go. Fear is real. Never forget that fear is real. The question is how can we overcome being victims of fear.

Let's take a brief look at the disciples on the Sea of Galilee at midnight and see how they dealt with fear. The disciples were out on the Sea of Galilee at midnight when they looked up and saw Jesus walking on the water. The disciples were afraid. Who would expect to see anyone walking on the water anytime but in the midst of a storm? I am sure it was like the show Fear Factor and the disciples weren't ready to play. Listen to what Jesus said to them. Take courage. It's me walking on the water. Fear propelled Peter out of the boat. He knew what the storms could do. He knew that the storm could kill. But out of this fear Peter took a gigantic step of faith. At the beginning of every act of faith there is a seed of fear.

Peter's story is encouraging to anyone that has failed-and that's all of us. God knows what's stuffed in our closets and underneath our beds. He knows about our worst actions and mistakes before we even committed them.

God also knows the best about you. He has given each of us certain gifts that we might be able to minister to each other with His love flowing through us. And just as he did with Peter, God wants to strengthen you to accomplish important ministries that others might be set free. You have the potential to be stronger as you become a victor and not a victim of abuse. Perhaps like Peter we can learn that we cannot follow Jesus in our own strength. We must realize that it is not self-reliance that God wants but total obedience and submission to Him.

But listen to what Peter says! "Lord if it's you, command me to come to you on the water." It was a tremendous act of faith! When fear overwhelms us would we have that kind of faith just to step out of our circumstances and trust Jesus? What convinces you that getting to God is better than sitting in your fear, analyzing every possible solution to the problem?

Peter was convinced to get out of the boat and start to walk towards Jesus; and even though you know the rest of the story, he still acted in faith. He still called out to Jesus, "Save me." Of the twelve disciples, Peter was the only one that took a step of faith. Do you have that kind of faith to step out of your circumstances and just trust God to provide?

As Christians we must have faith in God. Faith and not fear needs to be the core of our lives. When you take the first step to walk in faith, he will meet you at your need and carry your burdens. He holds all things together. He never has lost control. He fits the pieces together just like a puzzle. He never allows us to suffer without any good coming from it; somehow, some way He will always use the pain. We will walk through it and bring hope and strength to someone else. He takes all that would seek to destroy us in this life; sickness, disease, anxiety, abuse, despair, brokenness, fear and He heals. He delivers, sets us free and gives us hope.

Psalm 27: 1-3

Even if an army encamp against me, I shall not be afraid: And if war should rise against me, yet will I trust. One thing I have asked of the Lord, which I will seek: That I may dwell in the house of the Lord forever. For He will hide me in His shelter in the day of trouble, and set me high upon a rock

Unbelief and fear will keep us from doing what God has called us to do. It will hinder us from surrendering and having sweet peace as God steps in and carries us through the storms. Fear of being on a television program when my first book came out kept me up for hours the night before I had to go. I was afraid of saying the wrong thing, afraid of crying, afraid of answering questions and as crazy as it seems afraid of any of my friends seeing the program. Fear kept me very guarded about what I spoke about.

Fear isn't necessary sin, or failure, or even disobedience, it's all about danger and feeling threatened. Our enemy, Satan knows he has the victory if we don't confront our fear. The biggest secret of winning against fear is to acknowledge it and accept help from God. It is written in Isaiah 59:19, "When the enemy shall come in like a flood, the Spirit of the Lord will lift up a standard against him and put him to flight."

Today, I encourage you to ask yourself, have you seen God's hand at work in the troubles in your life? There is no reason our minds should be overwhelmed with fear when God is in control. Fear is a mask that we wear that keeps us from moving forward. No-one could see how afraid I was. I could say all the right words, be funny and brave and strong except when the lights were turned down low or completely off. It was then I lay trembling in fear. Will it happen again? It happened again and again. At first I was too young to understand what was happening, and I was terrified. I thought it was all my fault. I lived in constant fear, felt dirty and ashamed. The little girl who loved to play with her dolls, baking in her make-belief kitchen lost her sense of direction and joy. She spent many hours running from the conflicting fears and blaming herself. She felt unworthy and began to distrust every male figure in her life.

Every one of us carries emotional baggage from the past that impacts our decisions. If our past was filled with rejection, or if we didn't experience emotional or physical safety as children, then fear often becomes a stronghold in our lives. It is easy to say faith dispels fear and it is essential to pleasing God. But before faith can dispel our fears, can you trust God in the storms and believe what his word says about fear? We all battle fear. It is fear that keeps us from fulfilling the dreams God has placed in our hearts.

What steps do you need to take to face the fear that is controlling you? What kind of storm are you facing? Let it go, take that step through fear, and trust God. Hold to God's unchanging hand. Rely on His strength and see what God does. The greatest fear I deal with is that I will not be accepted if I take off the masks and speak the truth about sexual abuse. Will all my friends walk away from me if I speak the truth about what happened?

Let's take a look at what the scripture says concerning fear. Do you know that it has been said there is a scripture about fear for every day of the year?

> Psalm 27: 1
> The Lord is my light and my salvation whom shall I fear? The Lord
> is the stronghold of my life, of whom shall I be afraid?

I invite you to come along with me and take a walk. Abraham in faith took a hard walk. He believed that God would provide a sacrifice instead of him sacrificing his son. Moses and the Israelites took a long walk in the desert for forty years but when the night came that God was going to deliver them, I am sure they all went to bed, wondering how they would cross the Red Sea. They knew the army of Pharaoh was closing in fast. Many of them probably didn't know how to swim, and the night was windy, the waters turbulent. Darkness covered the land. But God didn't need sunshine to create a path through the sea- not just any path but a dry path.

Joshua took a long walk around the walls of Jericho. Peter walked on water. Then there was the walk that Jesus took called the Via Dolorosa, the way of sorrow, carrying the cross, bearing our sins. As we look at these walks they all ended in victory. God provided a ram in place of Isaac. He provided everything the Israelites needed including freedom from slavery, and He gave Peter the strength to walk on water.

But the greatest of these walks is the walk Jesus took to Calvary. He carried the cross of sorrow for our redemption. God asks ordinary people, you and I to step out in faith, release the fear, and realize that He is the one that makes us adequate to complete what He has called us to do. God promises His presence. There is always a changed life when we say yes to God's call. Those who say no are changed too. They become a little harder, walk in fear dreading what is going to happen next and a little more resistant to His calling. What will be your decision, will you walk in fear of what man may do to you or put your hand in the hand of almighty God who promises never to leave or forsake you?

Can anything be more fearful then a little five year old girl being molested repeatedly? Fear cripples, faith enables us to step out. Obedience is no guarantee of being spared adversity. I believe there is something inside of us that tells us there is more to life than living and walking in fear. As we look into the unknown future, with no clear path or direction from God, we may become fearful. God knew we would have many fears. That is why I believe God included over 365 scriptures concerning fear in the Bible. Fear not; God will meet all our needs. God is our hope for the future. We can thank Him for the past and look toward the future. I have found that sometimes He takes us out of situations but many times He just takes us through them.

It's in the valley when I realize I don't have the strength to look upward, to reach out and trust Him that I am grateful for tears and the ability to cry. Psalms 30:5 "Weeping may remain for a night, but rejoicing comes in the morning." I know that anyone; man, woman, young, old, rich, poor, black or white, can call on the Lord, and He will answer and meet our every need.

If you have been or are still going through a difficult period in your life, if you have been crushed by some circumstance that you had no control over, or you have lost a loved one through death or divorce; just remember that the Lord is close to the brokenhearted. Why not look up and take refuge in Him?

I have not forgotten the pain of the past, or the physical or emotional scars that were placed upon my body, but I want to give God glory for bringing me through the fire of sexual abuse and rape. I want to walk in victory. Millions of people destroy their future by focusing on the past. I did this for over fifty years! Afraid to ditch the masks and allow anyone to see the total me. Don't let your past failures hinder your future or define you.

Many women hate themselves and have no self-confidence because they have been abused, raped, committed adultery, had an abortion or been divorced. The truth is I didn't like who I saw in the mirror or went to bed with. I could not be totally honest with anyone because a part of me was always hiding and living with fear. Therefore I had to develop alternate beings and disassociate from the real me- the scared little girl who was sexually abused for many years. I didn't know how to say no! I only wanted to run far away, find someone who loved me, and wouldn't hurt me. I wore my letter "A" on my forehead and never let anyone get close enough to me to know the real child that wanted to be loved.

Don't give up, God loves you just as you are. My prayer for you is that you might let God examine your heart, walk close by your side, hide you in the shadow of His love and turn your darkness into light. He can cause your pain to flee and then you can proclaim that you are free.

Psalms 34:17-18
The righteous cry out, and the Lord hears them; He delivers them from all their troubles. The Lord is close to the brokenhearted and saves those who are crushed in spirit.

He erases away the past with one word- forgiven and removes the pain from our lives. He dries the tears we have shed. Luke, chapter seven describes a woman who endured her shame publicly. When a woman who had lived a sinful life, heard that Jesus was at a Pharisee's home she brought an alabaster jar of perfume. And as she stood behind him at his feet, she began to wet his feet with her tears. Then she wiped them with her hair and poured perfume on them. Because of her love for Jesus, this woman was expressing her sorrow and grief with her tears. By weeping in prayer and faith, believers express to God what is in their hearts. We need to take off the mask of thinking we always have to be strong, that it is wrong to cry, and trust God with all of our fears and feelings that we might be instruments of healing for each other.

Real love and devotion to Jesus must come from our hearts and a deep aware-ness of our sinful condition. Christ's love for us was revealed in the Garden, when He said, "Not my will, but thine be done." He gave himself up to the cross that you and I might be forgiven and healed. Where you are in your love walk with the Lord?

God had a plan for my life and he has a plan for yours. His desire was not for us to suffer. God wants to heal your hurts. He will restore your relationships but you must call on Him, come and pray, and seek Him with all your heart. We are able to find God's plans when we surrender to Him. He redeems us from our past and gives us hope for the future.

Take a moment to picture this scene. Abraham finally has a son only for God to command him to sacrifice his only son. Abraham prepares the altar, clenches his teeth, lifts the knife in the air and tries to control his anguish. Do you think Abraham might had a moment of fear but he chose to obey God? Suddenly he hears a voice from heaven telling him not to touch his son. The Lord provided a ram for the sacrifice.

Is it too much for us to make the same choice to trust God? He rescues us from danger, and all we see is the difficulty of the rescue. Have you ever questioned whether God really cares about your circumstances? I know I have. The trials you are facing today are not too big for God to handle. In a difficult situation like Abraham faced, would we be able to trust God? How many times have we not fully trusted God to be our strength, to meet our needs? Do we rest in unshakable faith that nothing will happen to us outside of God's love and care?

Could it be that God is waiting for you to give Him the broken pieces of your dreams and shattered heart so that He can make something beautiful out of them? Exposing ourselves to the light and presence of God's love will uncover the dark places of our hearts and allow him to change it. Fear of the unknown will paralyze you. Do you see yourself through the eyes of the past or the words of others? Beware of seeing yourself through other people's eyes; everyone has an opinion but do they see beyond the masks we wear? It is much more real to see yourself through the eyes of God; then and only then will you see yourself as one who is totally and unconditionally loved.

> Find a place inside where there is joy and the joy will burn out the pain. (Joseph Campbell)

Life is beautiful and can be amazing, but sometimes it is difficult to recognize because you are surrounded by overwhelming and difficult circumstances. Have you ever asked yourself why can't I be normal like everyone else? But how do we define being normal? I want to be a stronger person, better equipped to weather the storms. I want to believe and be convinced everything will work out. Until you reach acceptance of who you are, acknowledge your pain and circumstances, then and only then can you come to terms with who God has created you to be. His love is unconditional, He loves you right where you are now and will continue to passionately pursue you.

Are you like me and point out all the obstacles or hurdles that you have to overcome rather than trust your Creator? If God has called us to do something, He believes in us. Set aside your doubt and fears and run the race God is calling you to. I still have days when I struggle, question God; but my rebuilt and renewed sense of confidence is now firmly leaning upon God. He is my source of strength, and my solid rock. In the midst of a whole lot of uncertainty and why questions; set your mind on the one certainty in life. God loves you and He is in control. God sees you and me as being free from whatever was in our past when we surrender to Him. I wasted so many years wearing a mask, believing the lies of Satan that the sins I committed and the sin of sexual abuse which I didn't choose could not be forgiven. One of the biggest dangers of sexual abuse is it creates guilt, shame, delusion, anger, and a sense of failure because we are unable to move past the pain. We fail to see who we really are, a precious child of God.

> Isaiah 12:2
> "Surely God is my salvation; I will trust and not be afraid. The Lord,
> the Lord himself is my strength and my defense; he has become
> my salvation."

I used to believe if God wanted something important done, He would ask someone who had it all together. You know those women who never have an emotional meltdown at the most inappropriate time. I asked God, "Why me?" and then I read the story of Rahab in the book of Joshua. It gave me hope that sometimes the best woman for God's job doesn't have a perfect life or even a perfect faith. In fact, God sometimes chooses women who have rough pasts to get a job done. Rahab was a prostitute. Now why would God direct Joshua and the two spies to the house of a woman who didn't have the best reputation? God must have looked beyond her occupation as a prostitute and saw a woman with the perfect disposition to do the most good. God does not see our past, He only sees our willingness to sacrifice and obey Him. Rahab's story tells me that although I have listed all the reasons why God can't use me; He sees beyond my past, my abuse, my addictions and still calls me to be a voice for the innocent children.

God often calls us out of our comfort zones to a place of radical obedience to Him. God began stripping me of all my self-imposed masks one by one. He isn't finished with me yet for there are days I pick up those masks and put them all back on, drag my feet, screaming and crying this is too hard God. Instead of letting the past define who I am, instead of building walls and being a prisoner within those walls, God was calling me to change the past and allow Him to turn what Satan had meant for evil into not only healing for me but others dwelling in the same prison. God sees our value, even if we can't see beyond the broken places in our lives.

I think of the story of Humpty Dumpty. It was one of my favorite nursery rhymes as a child. I often used this illustration to describe my life. I used to love to climb on my daddy's lap until the one day when everything changed. Why did my daddy do bad things to me? Like Humpty Dumpty my life was shattered. I had fallen off the wall, and putting the broken pieces of my life back together did not ever seem to be possible.

God is refining me by putting me into the fire of His correction, loving me through the mess of my life. He can take my brokenness and give it meaning that I might help others. God does not look at the things people look at, He looks at the heart. What does God see when He looks at you? Are you a broken vessel being filled with His love and willing to do whatever He calls you to do?

Fear controls. God heals and restores.

1. How do you face your fears?
2. Are you seeking to walk out of your comfort zone?
3. Are you troubled with flashbacks of the abuse?
4. What is your greatest fear and how can you overcome this fear?

RELEASING THE SHAME

My heart cries out to the little girl within me, the little girl who wanted to feel special, to be loved, not mistreated and abused. There must be something wrong with me. Something must be lacking in my relationship with my father and mother. I am not acceptable. I am not worthy to be loved. What I have done to cause my parents to abuse me? It is hard to know who you are when you learned to feel shame about having needs. The shame of the sexual and emotional abuse is not mine but belongs to my abusers.

Shame is defined as embarrassment, dishonor, and humiliation. We are made uncomfortable so that we won't speak about the abuse. Shame was never mine to claim but I embraced it as a way of life. Repeatedly I was instructed do not tell. It is important to realize that abuse and shame exist in the same environment. The only way out of shame is to talk about it. Many people who experience sexual abuse and rape believe that they caused it.

Sexual abuse turns your whole world upside down; you no longer feel safe and nothing makes sense. Blaming yourself for what you did or did not do makes you feel safe and somewhat in control. It's a way of saying I can stop it from happening again. And then, it happens again and again. We hide behind our performances and addictions; the wall of self-denial becomes a stronghold. We keep the shame hidden deep in our hearts, afraid to place the blame where it belongs. Shame is like a cancer eating away at our deepest desires to be loved. The shackles of shame keep us bound to the past unless we choose to speak up.

The messages we receive if we dare to tell are not believed. Words that are spoken to us cause us to doubt our sanity. You imagined it, you are a liar, and it was your fault.

We develop behaviors that almost make other people believe that the abuse is what we want. We want a close relationship with others but push them away. We become defensive if criticized, or we become people-pleasers. We punish ourselves with negative thoughts and destruction self-talk.

Ironically, the way out of shame is to talk about it with a trustworthy friend. But the question remains, who can we trust with our secrets? Who will they tell or will they even believe us? Shame and silence often continues into adulthood controlling the way we react to many situations in our lives. Loss of losing the sense of innocence so overwhelmed me I felt that I had to be the one that was at fault.

As I grew older, the shame only intensified as I hurt myself by cutting myself and wondering if I would bleed to death. I felt so unlovable that I became addicted to diet drugs, cleanliness, and desired to punish my father by being promiscuous. Nothing felt right, as I had no sense of self-confidence or self-esteem. Shame touched every part of my life and my ability to relate to others. Shame is likely one of the worst effects of sexual abuse.

Rebuilding a life after sexual abuse isn't easy or quick, but with hard work, and support, it can be done. It won't be easy at first. Often we do not realize how strong a hold a behavior or thought pattern has on us until we try to get rid of it. When you shut the gates of believing that the shame is yours to hold onto, it frees you to live in the present and not the past. No matter what your past held, God can change the future. Get rid of those things that have held you bound and place the blame where it belongs, on your abuser.

We must ask ourselves some hard questions and then answer them truthfully. Will you do this? I believe in you and know the path is difficult but God can change your past and give you hope, restore your self-esteem, and most of all set you free.

1. Who had the real power, you or your abuser?
2. Who originally initiated the abuse?
3. Did the person give you affection and gifts?
4. Did you really understand what was happening?
5. Are you willing to make the decision to place the blame where it belongs?
6. Will you accept that you are not responsible for your abuser's actions?
7. Do you believe you deserved the abuse?
8. Do you feel that you are basically unlovable?
9. Do you have a difficult time believing that someone can love you?

The shame and pain of betrayal that I bore in silence, Jesus had already taken away at the cross. I could not do it alone, and neither can you but I hear God calling you to a place of revealing the truth about your abuser. You are not the one who is guilty. Shout it out that God loves, delivers, sets us free.

BREAK THE SILENCE OF SHAME AND BE SET FREE.

Hosea 1:10
In the very place where they were once named Nobody, they will be named God's Somebody. (The Message Bible)

UNLEASH THE POWER OF ANGER

Anger is defined as annoyance, irritation, resentment, fury, and uncontrollable rage. It would appear that the longer the anger is allowed to simmer it becomes stronger and eventually uncontrollable. Anger that is constantly stuffed eventually causes emotional and physical distress to the one who is holding it in, or to the one who has instigated the situation. Anger is often initiated by the abuser. The child has no recourse to defend themselves, and no one to protect them. It seems like the abuser is in a win-win situation as the child is forced into sexual relationships beyond their control and warned to never speak of it.

For many years, anger controlled my life. At times my anger felt so strong, even destructive, and directed mostly at myself. Other times I lashed out in anger hurting others. Anger destroyed any love or affection I had for my parents. I was angry that I was not believed when I told my mother what was happening. Even to this day when I speak of my mother, I become angry that she failed to protect me. I was angry at my father because he got away with sexually abusing me. I have been angry at myself because I have had to live with the memories of the abuse. My heart aches when I think that at some point the molestation begin to feel good. God made us to be sexual beings but not to be used and abused.

When we identify that we are angry, we must search for the reasons why, and whom we are angry with. I am angry that my daddy chose to hurt and sexually abuse me. I am angry that my mother allowed the abuse and never intervened. I am angry that I never tried harder to resolve this issue. Anger burns within us and destroys us, not the offender. Anger is like a forest fire that destroys everything in its path.

Anger made me feel vulnerable because it seemed like no one cared about what was happening to me as a child. It seemed easier to suppress the anger to keep from being hurt. So I found myself drawing into darkness never learning that I had the right to be angry and say no. I journeyed deeper and deeper into depression, turning the anger of the abuse inward. I erected barriers, smothered the anger, and then lashed out at others who had nothing to do with the reason for the anger.

My anger concealed helplessness, pain, and fear. Sometimes I felt so out of control, driven by the need to confront, and scream just to release the pain of betrayal. Every word that I said, every action that I took I felt I must control just to survive. Anger has power to make me hate, to keep me from forgiving, and to destroy my life.

As a child I was often angry when I saw families that expressed healthy love for their children. Now when I hear about a child being abused, I just cry out in my heart, dear God, help that child and punish the abuser.

Anger does not have to be destructive but most often in sexual abuse it is. Anger can be a healthy emotion but we must realize why we are so angry and find an appropriate way to express the anger without hurting ourselves or others. When we are sexually abused we are angry that no one seems to care, angry because we don't know whom to trust, and that it seems like the abuser always gets away with destroying the life of a child. We often are angry with ourselves for having to live with the memories of the abuse, the flashbacks, and wish we had a way to confront the issues and make the perpetrator pay for the abuse.

Anger can cover a whole range of emotions-fear, sadness, weakness, and inadequacy. Because our anger many times drives people away, we can become self-destructive. We need to develop an awareness that anger is always around, it is not a sin to be angry.

Some signs of anger to be aware of are a tightness in the chest, increased heart rate and blood pressure. It is found in your actions- standing up, pacing around, clenched fists, and lashing out at anyone. In my life I almost always avoided any confrontation by simply shutting down. How can we respond rationally when we feel so controlled by the circumstances? Anger is like trees subjected to the stormy elements. A tornado will often uproot trees causing damage to anything within its path. When the storm rages all around us, and within us, anger is powerful and we must release it. Let it go. Anger is like a raging fire, indiscriminately destroying everything in its path. Surges of anger, despair and tears flow like the mighty waves of the sea; lashing out and destroying everything in its path. Likewise if we hold onto anger we will destroy our hopes of recovery. We will hurt those around us that do not even understand why we are angry.

The question is how can we constructively control our anger and yet release it? Anger can be very positive. It can provide the motivation for change and healing. If you think about the people who have changed our world, Martin Luther King and Gandhi, they have been motivated with righteous anger at the injustices they experienced and saw.

Victims of sexual abuse often appear in control while inside they are filled with rage and anger, at the abuser, the non- offending parent or relative, or even people in charge such as leaders in the church or schools. The victim is dealing with pain of betrayal, powerlessness, rejection, broken boundaries, unmet needs, and being asked to live with a false sense of identity.

Anger is particular frightening if you have been surrounded by conflict, and violence as a child. As a victim of abuse we must learn ways to process our anger without being further abused. We need to find a safe way to release the anger without being punished for being angry. This is difficult to do as we must trace where the anger stems from, then be able to find a safe way to release it.

Things to think about:
1. Do you feel that you have held your anger inside and at times inappropriately lashed out at someone who had nothing to do with the abuse?
2. In suppressing your anger, does it make you feel in control?
3. How does anger affect you physically?
4. What is your first response to anger?

THE REFINER'S FIRE PURIFIES

Let me take you back to a Judean village in ancient days. Inside a small court-yard under a blazing sun stands a refiner of metals. This man's hands are gnarled with age, and yet we find him rolling and fingering a lump of ore. His experienced eye knows that within this lump of metal, there is silver. He lays the lump on his worktable, and then builds a fire with great care. Soon the flames are rising in the pit. At the worktable he picks up his hammer and begins to crush the lump of metal into smaller pieces.   You and I are that lump of metal, crushed and tarnished but with God's refining power made pure as gold.

He pauses occasionally to study the fire. From time to time he places more fuel on the fire that is already blazing. When the fire is just right, he gathers up the broken pieces of ore and lays them in a small container of tempered pottery. We are the broken pieces which he desires to make whole. He places it in the fire and sits down beside it. He doesn't pick up a book and begin to read it like I often do when I am waiting for something to be accomplished. He knows he has a long day before him and he will carefully watch the fire and the metal he is working with as long as the metal is subject to the fire. He realizes that silver is too precious to be forsaken in the furnace, and too valuable to be ruined through inattention. We are too precious to God for him to allow us to be destroyed. Slowly the ore softens, and the silver with its greater density and lower melting point, liquefies first. This is not the end of the process, however. Now he adds bits of charcoal inside the pottery. He knows this will enhance the sheen of the silver. The carbon of the charcoal will keep the refined melt from reabsorbing oxygen from the air. God adds bits of encouragement into our lives as we walk through the fire. He encourages us to be courageous, to release the pain of the sexual abuse and be set free.

But this is not the end of the process. The refiner adds more fuel and applies more air from the bellows and more impurities rise to the surface of the mixture. Again the refiner carefully skims away the dross that rises to the top. At this point the refiner is able to observe a dim reflection of himself. As we deal with our anger, our fears, our disobedience, and attempt to forgive, the refiner patiently waits and watches, never leaving the metal unattended, never stepping away from the fire he has stoked to do the work. He is not satisfied until all the impurities are released, brought to the surface and exposed for what they are, and then skimmed off.

Finally the refiners' face breaks into a smile for as he gazes into the liquid silver his reflection is clearer. However, the work is not completed. More hours pass as he keeps the fire at just the right temperature, watching closely for that perfect moment, when he gazes into the silver, and sees a clear image of himself.

The refiner has taken what was dull and lifeless and made it beautiful. He has taken what was impure and made it pure. He has made the lump of ore that had potential value into something of great value.

What made the difference in this lump of ore? The fire, the relentless heat of the fire, under the watchful care and hand of the refiner. If the silver was left too long in the flames, it would be destroyed.

You ask, why do I tell you this story? Because you and I are more than observers in this story. We are the silver. God is the refiner. The fire is the fire of His making, for He longs to make us holy, righteous, and sees our value in His kingdom. He longs for us to be the light of this world; so the world as well as the principalities and powers, and all satanic hosts can behold the glory of the Redeemer working through us.

The fiery trials we have walked through, the abuse that has left us broken, the drugs that have left us addicted, and the sexual acts of fornication, rape, or molestation that have left us impure when put into the refiners' fire were never meant for our destruction. The fiery trials that became a part of our lives are momentary compared to eternity. If we allow the Great Refiner to skim the impurities out of our lives, we will make a difference in this world. Through it all, God has promised never to leave us; He is always there to make sure every flame that reaches us is the right temperature; not to hot that we might be destroyed but hot enough that we might feel the pressure and be changed by the hand of God.

A refiners' fire does not destroy indiscriminately like a forest fire, or consume like an incinerators' fire but it refines, purifies, and separates that which is not good for us and leaves us holy before our God. God leaves this work of creating us in His image to no other hands but His own. He may give his angels charge over us when we are in danger, but He always keeps our purification process beneath His ever-watchful eyes and hands. He is patient until the work is completed.

Psalms 66: 10-11
For you O' God, tested us; you refined us like silver.

The refiner's fire burns with a sacred heat, destroying that which has tarnished our lives. There burns a fire with sacred heat; white hot with holy flame; and all who dare pass through its' blaze will not emerge the same. Some as bronze, and some as silver, some as gold. All are hammered by their sufferings, on the anvil of His will but not destroyed.

I'm learning to trust His touch, to crave the fire's embrace, for though my past with sin was etched, His mercies did erase. Each time His purging cleanses deeper; I'm not sure that I will survive. Yet the strength in growing weaker keeps my hungry soul alive.

The Refiners' fire has now become my souls' desire. Purged and cleaned and purified that the Lord may be glorified. He is consuming my soul, refining me and making me whole. No matter what I may lose, I choose the Refiners' fire.

My question today to you is what do you choose; the refiners' fire that makes you holy or the fire of the destruction of sin? The choice is yours. What is keeping you chained to the past? I chose prescription drugs for over twenty-five years and have just recently been delivered from the hold of drugs on my life. I chose to attempt suicide many times but God rescued me. I chose to deal with my pain by putting on a mask everyday but God said it is time to take the masks off, release the past, forgive, and move on.

II Corinthians 4:17-18 gives us hope. For our light affliction, which is but for a moment, is working for us in a far more exceeding and eternal weight of glory; while we do not look at the things which are seen, but at the things which are not seen. For the things which are seen are temporary, but the things that are not seen are eternal.

Jesus is calling you to come to him face to face and pour out your heart to Him. He is your refuge, healer, and deliverer. Healing is a process not a microwaved incident in your life. If you desire to untangle the rope holding you to the past, or untangle the Christmas lights to put on the tree, it will take time. Jesus is waiting for you to make the first step, the first cry to Him, and He will help you.

Seek someone whom you can trust to tell your story to, be accountable to them, and ask them to pray for you. I was blessed with a wonderful Christian woman, trained to do sexual abuse counseling who volunteered to help me walk through many issues that stemmed from the sexual abuse. It takes someone with lots of compassion and patience to listen to our stories and help us to let go and become useful again. I asked God to microwave the process of healing in my life. He said I want to spend quality time with you so that you get it right this time. What a patient and awesome God we have!

Does this sound like your life right now? Are you alone, wandering around wondering why God doesn't just immediately deliver you? The Israelites were enslaved in Egypt for over 400 years and wandered in the wilderness for over forty years but God did deliver them. Their deliverance was definitely not microwaved!

I know there are days when the plan of God seems completely wrong, and we simply don't understand it. But before the world began, before you or I were conceived, God had a plan for our life. We were destined to be the temple of God, and God's Spirit would reside within us. Today I chose the Potter's wheel, the refiner's fire instead of the fire of the sexual abuse; instead of the fire of anger and unforgiveness that I experienced. What will you choose?

Things to think upon:
1. Where are you in your walk of recovery?
2. Are you still in the fire being restored?
3. Do you understand God's plan for your life?
4. What will you choose-to stay hidden or be healed?

I AM

Experiencing the river of God today as I sit at his feet
Encountering Jesus, the awesome power of His blood
His overwhelming love, is touching me, healing me
Taking the broken pieces making me completely whole.
I AM
Broken in His presence, wonderful counselor is He
I am precious in His sight, at last I can claim victory
I come drinking, thirsting for living water
At the fountain of life, seeking His amazing love
I Am
Reclaiming the territory, abandoned by the enemy
Confident am I that the broken, cracked vessel
I place in the Master's hand, can be made holy,
Completely restored by the love of the Master.
I Am
Overwhelmed by His love, His complete forgiveness
A wounded healer, refined by the fire of His holiness
I am a drink offering, willing to be poured out to the captives
Sent to the broken spirits, binding up the wounds
Of my Saviors' beloved women, you and I.

WILL THE REAL ME
PLEASE STAND UP?

What does it mean to be real? It means to be genuine, trustworthy, and sincere. I could be counted on to do what I said I would do but God showed me areas of my life that needed to be repaired. There was a part of my heart that was black, hardened, and needed to be broken before God's comfort could come. I didn't ask for mercy, but mercy was freely given to me.

I asked myself, will the real me please stand up? That reminded me of the book Velveteen Rabbit that I used to read to children.

Let's take a look at the book Velveteen Rabbit, written by Margery Williams. You may remember that the story begins on a Christmas morning. A little boy discovered a velveteen rabbit in his Christmas stocking, the very same rabbit that he had seen in a storefront window. Like many children the rabbit was loved for a couple of hours until the little boy received more expensive toys that boasted about being fashioned after real things. But the little rabbit didn't know that there was such a thing as a real rabbit. But one night the little rabbit discovered Skin Horse who was worn but wise. He had lived longer in the nursery than any of the other toys.

The poor little rabbit felt so sad and insignificant. He asked the wise Skin horse, "What is real? Must I have something that buzzes inside of me and a stick out handle?" The wise old Skin Horse said, real isn't how you are made. It's something that happens to you when a child loves you for a long, long time. He doesn't want to just play with you but he really loves you just for who you are. Then you become real. The Velveteen rabbit asked Skin Horse, Does it hurt to become real? The wise old Skin Horse replied sometimes but it really doesn't matter for when you are real you don't mind being hurt. Does it hurt to be honest about the sexual abuse and rape? Yes, it does but each time I talk to someone, a little more of the fear and pain is released. And then, a little more healing comes into my life.

When someone loves you right where you are each time it gets a little easier to share the pain. God interrupted my life by placing me in a relationship of love and accountability to a dear friend. I spend a day with my friend Alice as she asked me many questions about the abuse. Her only request was that I not lie to her. I tried to tell her what happened but when she asked me if my father had raped me, I said no. I wouldn't talk to her for a few weeks because I had lied to her. Finally I confessed to her that I had lied about being raped but she said she already knew that. She just wanted me to be honest with her and speak openly about the issues that were troubling me. Being real is more than just talking about the good things, it's about sharing the pain. I was so conditioned to never talk about the abuse that I really didn't know how to be real.

Sometimes, we are like the velveteen rabbit, we don't know how to be real, or have the courage to speak the truth about our lives. Fear keeps us immobilized. We are afraid of what others will think of us if we reveal the whole story of our abuse, or of our marriage that is failing because of adultery, or the abortion we had when we were a teenager. We hide behind closed doors as we try to deal with our pain by using drugs or alcohol, or by lying or being evasive with our mask of self-protection tightly in place. I became a pro at being evasive, changing the subject, or laughing when someone asked me what is wrong with you.

We wear a different mask when we are with our friends that drink or do drugs. We attend church with our self-righteous mask in place. We try to be the perfect Christian without really knowing that God can deliver us and heal us. It's one thing to be real with God but can we be real with those we are the closest to? Can we admit that we need help? Admitting our need is the first step in recovery. Can we not only allow others to tell us their story but tell them our story? It is getting easier each day to speak of the things that trouble me or cause me to be depressed, but I used to only listen to other people's stories and try to help them without telling them my story.

God knew the real me before I even knew myself. He knew what would happen in my life. He saw the abusive father and mother I had and wept because of the physical and emotional scars they placed upon my life. He loved me just as I was, a scared little girl that was used to hiding and afraid of being real enough to tell anyone what was happening in her home. He didn't condemn me when I attempted to kill myself and cried out in anger to Him. He just loved me. I was a broken vessel and thought I had no redeeming value in God's eyes, but He took the brokenness and cleansed me with His love and forgiveness. God never sees us as throw away people. As children of God, we are more precious, beautiful and valuable than we can ever comprehend.

Romans 8:31-33
If God be for us, who can be against us? He who did not spare His own son, but gave him up for us all, how will He not also, along with him, graciously give us all things? Who will bring any charge against those whom God has chosen? It is God who justifies.

To be real the masks must come off. Unfortunately at times I pick up one of those masks I have discarded, put them back on again but it doesn't fit as securely as before. God doesn't necessarily expect us to be healed immediately. It seems kind of strange that we should want to take off the mask and go through the pain of pruning the past from our lives, doesn't it? It reminds me of working out when we say "no pain, no gain. It seems to be a never ending process as I often crawl back into my safe place, grab one of those masks hiding the real me.

We must desire and make the choice to be healed. Yes, I experienced the horror of sexual abuse and rape. I became addicted to prescription drugs, walked in shame and fornication, unable to forgive my abusers. An addiction is something that controls us, something that we feel we cannot do without. I ran from the pain using prescription drugs thinking I was better than the woman or man who used street drugs. Like any addict, I needed a fix when things became rocky. I needed to feel accepted, and did whatever was necessary to be affirmed. Would somebody just love me enough to reach out and care if I am real?

I experienced many emotional problems unable to relate to people without a mask on. I became good at avoiding the truth. A friend once asked me if avoiding speaking the truth was considered a lie. I thought about it for a moment and realized at least in my life it was a lie. I could not function well in a close relationship for any length of time. I didn't want people to see the real me, the woman whose heart was breaking. Would they still love me? Could I be real?

The walls we face might be emotional or even relational, but God desires to tear every wall down. He will not condemn you if you fail many times trying to overcome the situations in your life. He will only pick you up, set you on your feet, and encourage you to try again. Healing and overcoming addictions is a process. It cannot be microwaved. It has taken me almost three years to get to where I am now.

But one day God said enough is enough. He called me away from all the addictions, the shame and blame game. He didn't want me to simply forget the pain of the past, let the scars heal over and never reach out to others. We can't change our past but what we do with it can help others to be released from their pain. We are God's hands and feet, His mouth speaking the truth to minister to others. I spent years wondering if my past or the failures of the present had stolen my value in God's eyes.

Luke 12:6-7

"Are not five sparrows sold for two pennies? Yet not one of them is forgotten by God, indeed the very hairs of your head are all numbered. Don't be afraid, you are worth more than many sparrows"

Jesus sees us as a precious treasure. In biblical times, sparrows had little value, other than being cheap food for the poor. Jesus shared with His disciples how God loved the little sparrows, even though they were worthless in the eyes of the world. How much more does He love you and me? Jesus sees beyond our masks, our imperfections, sins and fears, and beholds us as being valuable. He takes our imperfect life and gives us great value. No matter what we have done or has been done to us; He loves us simply because He created us and we are His. Our value does not only make us precious to God, but it also takes all imperfections and makes them useable for amazing purposes of ministering unto others. I struggle daily with low self-esteem, a poor image of myself, feelings of unworthiness; but God takes what I have to give and multiplies it that others might see His love.

There is in each of us some deep need, question, hurt, or unhealed pain. This need may have driven us to a life of drugs, alcohol, food addictions, depression, and even to attempted suicide. No doctor or psychologist can heal that need. We can't do it by looking for some emotional answer, or by reading self-help books. No pastor, friend, or even our mate can meet the inner need that will give us the courage to stand up and be real. No one can get to the root of it because they don't have the ability or know the whole story. There are people with vast amounts of wealth who continue to search for answers. You can't find help for your need anywhere else in the world but through Christ. We must trust him and shout it out that he is God our deliverer and breaks every chain sets us free.

There is no other hope. You have to make the decision that your need is spiritual. You can't just hear the truth, you have to act on it. Jesus Said, "I am the way, the truth, and the life. If you love me, you will obey me. You will do what I say. Everything you need is met in Jesus. Acknowledge your need, and take off all the masks you have been wearing. Being real is having the courage to take down the walls we have put up, realize the walls we think are there to protect us are really keeping us in bondage.

God sent His son Jesus who paid the price that our broken lives can be restored. His scars could have been healed but He chose to leave the scars and that is how the disciples recognized Him. He bore your shame and mine as the soldiers mocked Him. His scars are for our redemption.

What will you do with your scars?

For over fifty years, I never let anyone know I was sexually abused. I walked in shame, anger, and un-forgiveness and was unwilling to share the pain of my childhood and youth. It was my secret until one day God exposed my secret. He said, "My child I want a more intimate walk with you. It is time to reveal your pain and be real. I am calling you to a closer walk with me. Do not continue to hide behind your fear for I have a greater work for you to do." He said, "Be a voice for the innocent. My children are hurting."

Even in the midst of pain, the loss of a loved one, we can still lift our voices and sing Jesus loves me. It is a child's song, and yet the message is clear. Jesus loves me, this I know for the Bible tells me so. It is this unconditional love that sustains us and calls us to minister to others.

I cried out to God, Why me? I am not qualified! What will people think? God, is there not something else that you want me to do? Something that is safe and would bring glory to your name. God remained quiet and didn't answer.

His answer was clear when He begin to bring others into my life that told their stories of abuse. I listened and prayed with them but didn't share my story. It was then that God again said unto me, "Do not be afraid, be a voice for the innocent. My children are hurting." I did not know if I could be that vessel of healing, compassion, and love God was calling me to be. He spoke to my heart once again telling me that He would be with me. Do not fear for I will never leave you.

No matter what your struggle has been or still is, victory is possible. However most of us don't think that it is possible. We forget to acknowledge each little success. I like the way 2 Peter chapter 1: 5-7 says "We are to add some things to our faith such as self-control and perseverance. It reminds me of when I was having occupational and physical therapy three times a week. We must exercise our muscles to make them effective and strong. Each added exercise seemed to be a struggle, but ultimately I realized each exercise was a victory towards getting well. Each time I made a decision to exercise, I got stronger. Sometimes victory seems so far away because we measure it by the end goal. To win the race, we must overcome the fear of falling and run until we know we are victorious.

Healing is a process, it cannot be microwaved. You must first recognize that you have a wound that needs healing, then be willing to disclose that wound and be truthful first to yourself and then to someone you can be accountable to. I find being real is very difficult for me as I have kept so many things hidden for years. So many times we want to run from our problems, blame everyone else, without realizing we need to accept what happened and move forward from there. For years I did not even acknowledge that I been sexually molested and raped. Healing comes with acknowledging the wound and applying the truth of God's Word to our lives. God is our deliverer and breaks every chain.

Will you and I be ashamed to show our scars to a hurting world? Will we proclaim the healing of our wounds that others might have the victory and peace that only God can give? Jehovah Rapha, the one who heals, can transform our wounds into beautiful scars so that we might be able to help others to the road of recovery.

God takes our broken hearts and pursues us relentless with His unconditional love and mercy. Because of what Jesus did on the cross we are clothed with His righteousness. His sacrifice was complete and full of love for us.

Isaiah 43:1-2
Fear not, for I have redeemed you; I have summoned you by name;
you are mine. When you pass through the waters, I will be with you,
and when you pass through the rivers, they will not sweep over you.
When you walk through the fire, you will not be burned, the flames
will not set you ablaze. For I am the Lord your God.

God expresses his love and protection for his people. How many times have we come close to death and not even realized it? He is the perfect protector. His word says that he delivers us and saves us from our enemies. He is our stronghold and will hold us cradled in His hands. Because God loves you and me so much, our pain becomes His pain. The scars were placed upon my body and Jesus wept. At the same time He bore my scars and shame at the cross. Every praise belongs to Him; He is the Lord of my life.

Isaiah 61:3
You promised beauty for ashes, the oil of joy for mourning, the
garment of praise for the spirit of heaviness.

I didn't know what true love was or how to be emotionally healed. The wound of a child feeling unwanted, rejected, and sexually abused is a wound that goes so deep into the heart of the child that the child ends up being an adult that feels worthless and doesn't have the ability to love. Sexual abuse is an invasion of a child's heart and soul and most often comes from someone who should be protecting the child. The after effect is that the child does not know who to trust or to reach out to for love and protection. I was that child, unable to love and trust anyone. But God loved me, and promised to heal every hurt I had ever endured.

He will replace the violence with healing and give you victory. He will replace rejection with acceptance, isolation with His presence, and low self-esteem by giving you the power to be an overcomer. The power of evil around you is no match for the power of Jesus in you.

When I became a Christian, I was dealing with brokenness, sexual abuse, and the loss of my husband. I read many self-help books but I did not have the power or strength to heal myself. I didn't have to earn God's love; He was only waiting for me to accept what He had already done. When we accept His unconditional love, it changes us. Jesus came to heal our hurting hearts, we cannot do it alone.

Jesus came to set the prisoners free, and to heal the brokenhearted. Do you think that quite possibly the crowd was shocked by the words of Jesus. They expected a mighty warrior, a King, not a heart surgeon. But He came that we might be made whole. I came to Christ broken expecting Jesus to make me whole, but still trying to do it in my own strength. The power of the cross does not come through what I can do, but through what Jesus has already done for me. My hurting heart sent me running down pathways that I now regret. I was searching for love and deliverance in all the wrong places.

WHAT GOD DID FOR ME, HE WILL DO FOR YOU.

He took me from my brokenness into a realm of love. He bound up my love-starved heart and replaced it with a new heart filled with His love. Through this process I learned I didn't have to earn God's love. I came to Him with all my baggage, fears, and regrets, and He replaced them with His boundless love. He is the one person we can be totally real with and He will not condemn us.

In the place of our greatest shame and self-condemnation, our most significant act of spiritual warfare is choosing to believe God still loves us. Try as I might, I cannot grasp just how deep and perfect God's love is for me. I simply cannot wrap my mind around that kind of love. He lives in me, knows everything about me, including my deepest desires and darkest secrets and yet He still loves me. He understands perfectly all the things that happened in my life including the things which are still to come or to be revealed to me. His love is boundless. Jean Anouilh says "Our entire life- consists ultimately in accepting ourselves as we are" Being fully me is so much better than being an imitation of someone else.

I urge you to open your heart to receive vast amounts of His love. The more of His love that is in your heart, the less room there is for fear. Perfect love (God's love) casts out all fear. Where have you come from and where are you going? If you are like me you may think it's easier to keep the masks on and run from our problems, and sidestep accountability. Accountability is not just being responsible to someone; for we can still wear our masks and not be trustworthy. It is a process of being honest and vulnerable for your actions to someone you can trust to speak the truth into your life; and when you mess up you take responsibility for your actions. IT IS ABOUT BEING REAL!

Questions to think about and answer honestly:
1. What are you hiding?
2. Can you identify why you have kept quiet?
3. What keeps you in bondage?
4. List the things you would need to do to become real and be healed.

YOU ASK ME TO FORGIVE MY ABUSERS?
LOOK AT WHAT GOD DID!

Here I am Lord just sitting before you with a heart that is broken into tiny little pieces finding it difficult to believe that you can or have forgiven me. I know your word says if we ask for forgiveness that we are forgiven but if I hold unforgiveness in my heart how can I ever believe you have forgiven me? I have tried so hard to let go of the bitterness, hatred, and forgive those who abused me but if I have forgiven why is there still so much conflict in my heart?

I feel so broken, so lost. I have asked you to forgive me again and again but your word says if we can't or won't forgive those who have sinned against us, then you do not forgive us. Will the pain ever truly be gone so that I can minister to others honestly? Why is it so hard to forgive?

One reason we resist forgiving is because we really don't know how it works. Most of us assume if we forgive our offenders they get to go on their merry ways while we suffer from their actions. While God commands us to forgive others he never tell us to keep trusting those who violate our trust. Forgiveness is not based on other's actions but on our attitude. Even if they never ask, we must be willing to forgive, let go, and move on.

Is it because I want to judge my abusers and expect them to pay a penalty for rejecting and abusing me? Or is it because I feel that such sins as abuse are "unforgiveable?" Who am I to judge? JESUS, you even have the power to forgive the sin of unforgiveness. I cry out to you today, Lord, is it because I haven't accepted your authority to forgive my abusers? Do I even deserve forgiveness? For me to say that something is unforgiveable is to limit the power and authority of Jesus. If I keep the whole law and stumble in one point I am guilty of breaking the whole law.

Your word says before you judge someone else, stop and think about all God has forgiven you for. My heart breaks as I think of all the things my father made me do while my mother watched. Yet they asked for your forgiveness and I have to believe that you forgave them. I have tried so hard to forgive them but the pain of the flashbacks cause me to cry out in anger. YET AS I STUDY YOUR WORD I READ THE WORDS "FOR IF YOU FORGIVE OTHERS FOR THEIR TRANSGRESSIONS, YOUR HEAVENLY FATHER WILL ALSO FORGIVE YOU." The expectation in this scripture is simple; if we will forgive others in the same way that we have been forgiven by God, we will be set free. Jesus placed a high importance on the subject of forgiveness. I believe that there are times when we may not feel like forgiving someone. It is at that time we must express that we are willing to forgive. What it comes down to is allowing love and forgiveness to cover their sins and ours, thus destroying bitterness. When we practice love and forgiveness we become protected against another's offence. Then when someone sins against us we do not have to search for forgiveness, it is already available.

When everything in you wants to hold a grudge, point a finger, and remember the pain, God wants you to lay it all aside. That is where I want to be, always ready to forgive and be forgiven. Everything is possible with God.

No stone is left unturned when we submit to Him. Are you and I forgiving totally, completely, and unconditionally? That is how Jesus forgives us- nothing held back. That is when an unexpected peace surrounds us when we have laid it all at the feet of Jesus. If we desire that intimate walk with God he will show us all of the areas in our lives where we are walking in disobedience to Him. He loves us that much! The mask of unforgiveness has to go for I have been forgiven much.

Forgiveness needs to come from your heart not just your mouth. I just want to give you an illustration I read today on forgiving from the heart. As we all know squirrels often bury their nuts in the ground for later use. This works well for the squirrels except sometimes they forget where they left their nuts. The results are predicable- the nuts they buried so carefully sprout and grow. Half-hearted forgiveness works the same way as we continue to hold on to bitterness and anger. It becomes harder to let go of the bitterness and it creates within us a poisonous situation which taints our lives and the lives of those we associate with.

The Lord spoke to my heart today telling me that refusing to walk in forgiveness is very small in comparison to the sins I have been forgiven for. It is as if we are attempting to play god, choosing whom we will forgive and will not forgive. We may even feel justified in our unforgiveness but Jesus instructs us that we must show mercy in the same way that He had mercy on us. I cannot continue to believe that FORGIVENESS IS OPTIONAL OR DEPENDENT UPON THE SITUATION.

Forgiveness must be from the heart, genuine and complete. If it isn't then we are like the squirrels hiding nuts and presenting an appearance of forgiveness but in reality hiding some part of unforgiveness. Today the Lord showed me that one way of hiding unforgiveness is by thinking, "I'll forgive but I won't forget. I have been guilty of this and it becomes obvious that I did not forgive the same way God forgave me- without reservation and unconditionally.

There is no greater example than Jesus. He was physically abused, mocked, wore a crown of thorns and condemned to be crucified. In the midst of all this abuse Jesus prayed, "Father forgive them, for they do not know what they are doing." How can I do any less? God's offering of forgiveness was paid before we even recognized that we needed to be forgiven. We must forgive even if the person is guilty of the worst kinds of sin. We must forgive even if they never asked to be forgiven. By doing that we prevent weeds of bitterness from growing in our hearts and provide a way for others to be able to see that forgiveness and love must be given in the smallest of offences up to those attacks that shatter our lives.

We have talked about forgiving others but if we fail to forgive ourselves we are saying that the blood of Jesus is not enough, that our sin is unforgiveable.

We do not have the right to hold on to something which Jesus has cleansed us from. I know that I must let it go. It's the only way for me to be completely free. Unforgiveness is like being held in a prison cell from which there is no escape even though the doors are wide open. We make the choice to stay imprisoned by our attitude. Yes, there are times we are so deeply wounded and we cannot talk about it, but God is greater than any circumstance we have survived. His love is so vast that he wants us to be restored and healed. God has opened the prison doors of my heart. I must make the choice to walk through those doors and let go of the past. He's calling you and me to break every chain that holds us to the past. The Bible says forgiveness is the willingness to cover the sins of another, and the willingness to pay a price for redemption. It is seeking reconciliation with the offender and restoring a broken relationship.

God didn't create you or me just to go through the motions of existing. He doesn't want us to just exist in a survival mode. He wants to set us free, to praise him and have victory over the past. When we forgive, God gives us freedom so we are no longer shackled by our anger.

I know this is true because for many years I tried to serve God in my own strength, with stinky thinking, and believing I had to be in control. Because I was unwilling or didn't know that forgiveness wasn't just saying I'm sorry, I was losing the battle in my mind and listening to the voice of the enemy. Break through happens when we realize we must be surrendered completely to God and let go of the past.

In the very beginning of my walk with the Lord and throughout the years it seemed like I was constantly being reminded that I must forgive my abusers. God was patient even when I cried out that they didn't deserve forgiveness. Why should I forgive? I had done nothing wrong.

Let me give you some reasons why it is hard to forgive.
1. We don't understand how much we have been forgiven.
2. We believe we must forgive instantly.
3. We believe that if we forgive and forget that we must tolerate the transgressions done unto us.
4. Many times reconciliation is confused with forgiveness.

Let's take a brief look at the woman caught in adultery. The teachers of the law and the Pharisees brought in a woman caught in adultery. They made this woman stand before the group and told Jesus that this woman was caught in the act of adultery. They went on to tell Jesus that in the Law of Moses that this woman should be stoned to death. Obviously they had no mercy or forgiveness in their hearts. Then they dared to ask Jesus what He would do or say about this situation. Jesus did not answer them at this point. He simply bent down and started to write on the ground with His finger. When they kept on questioning Him, he straightened up and said to them, "If anyone of you is without sin, let him be the first to throw a stone at her."

Before today I would not have compared myself to these teachers and Pharisees. But as I look back on my walk with the Lord I have committed this same type of judgment having no mercy and compassion for my parents or those addicted to drugs. Although I never did "Street drugs" I was just as guilty by taking a prescription drug that is used on the street. For over twenty years I "coped" with the abuse by taking prescription drugs.

I attended church faithfully, but it seemed like there was always a chamber of my heart that was hidden from everyone. The pain was too great to share. I didn't want to forgive so I was existing only in a survival mode still bound to the things of the past. It has not been a onetime decision but an everyday battle of my mind and heart to reach the place of forgiveness. We must forgive totally and unconditionally. That is how Jesus forgives us. Forgiveness is not only based on the words we speak but our attitude. We must make the choice to forgive even though the other person never asks for forgiveness.

Later, we see Jesus with the Samaritan woman. She said to Jesus you are a Jew and I am a Samaritan women. How can you ask me for a drink?" Jesus answered her. "If you knew the gift of God, and who asks you for a drink, you would have asked Him and He would have given you living water." Let me tell you the end of this story. The woman left her water jug and went back to town and said to the people. "Come and see a man who told me everything I ever did." Could this be the Christ? Because of one woman's testimony, many of the Samaritans went to check this man out and believed in Him. Then they came back and said to the women, "We no longer believe just because of what you said; now we have heard for ourselves and we know that this man really is the Savior of the world. It is no longer possible for me just to speak the truth and not walk in it. My story will be believed when I walk the path I am declaring to others.

One of the most difficult steps we must take is to forgive our abusers. Your abuser does not have the right to control or manipulate, or to condemn you for your actions. Nor do they have the right to define your relationships with others or demand that you have a relationship with them only. This makes it difficult for us to forgive. It also makes it difficult for us to surrender to God and realize His love is not the kind of love that controls but delivers and heals us. God says we must forgive and without God's forgiveness we all would be lost.

Why is it so easy for some people to judge and condemn others when they have a beam in their own eye? Then I stop and think why is it difficult for me to just accept God's grace and mercy and not let others condemn me? It was easy for me to doubt that God could redeem the pain. I could not see myself as God saw me. I often compared myself to a puzzle and some of the pieces were missing and could not be found. He called me a child of God while I thought of myself as a slave to sexual abuse and drugs. He called me righteous but I only saw myself guilty of sin. He called me to exercise my authority over the enemy, but the power of sexual sin and guilt kept me bound with chains that I did not have the strength to break.

Walking in forgiveness is absolutely necessary, not only for our abusers but for ourselves. For many years I verbally stated I had forgiven my abusers- my father, brothers, mother and two other men that sexually abused me. Yet I still harbored unforgiveness in my heart. It seemed like there was no way to let go of the disgrace and pain that surrounded me. I didn't really think they deserve forgiveness. My life was a mess because of their actions. At one point in my walk with the Lord I wanted them to go to hell. I cried out to God to help me to forgive not only those who abused me but to forgive myself.

After hearing a message one night at church about forgiveness I cried all night and didn't return to church for a few weeks. I had a difficult time believing that God would ever forgive me when my heart cried out for revenge. I bowed my head and begin to weep and to pray with total honesty to a loving God that was willing to forgive me. I cried out to God with a heart that was overwhelmed with sorrow; for at times the sexual abuse brought pleasure. At times as a teenager I allowed sexual advances because I wanted to know if the pleasure was real or just a result of being abused for so long. There were layers of pain and issues I'd never dwelt with. Like most people I didn't want to face the pain. Finally I realized that carrying around unforgiveness never affected my abusers. I was the one who was putting poison in my body and creating all kinds of illness. My parents never did ask for forgiveness or even admit that what they had done was wrong. I had to choose to forgive, and leave the past behind.

Eventuality I finally realized that forgiveness is not saying that what happened to me was right. It is simple saying we are not responsible for their actions. In making the decision to forgive we are no longer allowing ourselves to be held in bondage. Giving forgiveness releases us to move forward.

William P. Young says in his book "The Shack", you may have to declare your forgiveness a hundred times a day the first day and the second day, but the third day will be less and each day after, until one day you will realize that you have forgiven completely."

Will you believe that God can change your life? Will you tell your story that others might have hope and deliverance? I tell my story simply because there are women that need to know that they do not have to live with the darkness and shame of sexual abuse, rape, and adultery. I finally realized it was all about letting go and the issue of trust. All relationships are built on trust. Some people put their trust in money, others in education but without God they continue to live in the past. When we are going through the storms of life, the Great Physician has a prescription. You do not have to go to the local drugstore to get it filled. You will not have to pay exorbitant amounts of money. It is free. He only asks us to surrender to Him.

God asks one thing of man- that man should trust Him. He does not ask for payment, His son paid the price. Trust and obey for there is no other way. Trust is not emotional; it's based on knowledge that God is faithful. When we put our trust in God, no matter what the crisis, what our sin, or what our heartache is, we are forgiven by trusting in the blood of Jesus. We have hope for the future because we trust He is all powerful and forgiving. Some people put their trust in money, then the stock market crashes or the bank closes or the interest rates of IRA's drop so low you might as well spend the money. Others put their trust in education and still can't get a job.

When we are going through one of life's storms, we need an advocate that will stand with us. I urge you to trust in the Lord with all your heart. Lean not on your own understanding. Proverbs 3:5

Let me give you a visual illustration of trust. I read this in a book. A farmer went to the county fair and saw a sign that read Airplane rides for $50.00. Now the farmer really wanted to ride in that plane but he told the pilot the price was too high. The pilot said, "I'll make you a deal. If you trust me enough to ride without screaming, the ride is free. If you scream the price is double." The farmer and his wife agreed to the deal. The pilot took off and took the plane through a series of acrobatic maneuvers. After the plane landed, the pilot said to the farmer. I'm amazed you didn't scream once. The farmer replied, "I almost screamed on that barrel roll when my wife fell out."

No matter what the circumstances that have you bound, God can give you a beautiful future. When Job's family was killed, his home destroyed, and his crops and health destroyed, he could have blamed God and cursed him. But God blessed him and gave him back double what he had lost. When David a man after God's heart sinned and committed adultery, God was waiting for David to repent.

Paul reminds us what God expects of us and what our eternal goals should be.

> 2 Corinthians 4:6-10
> For God, who said, "Let light shine out of darkness" may his light shine in our hearts to give us the light of the knowledge of God's glory displayed in the face of Christ. For we have this treasure in jars of clay to show that this all surpassing power is from God and not from us. We are hard pressed on every side, but not crushed, perplexed, but not in despair, persecuted, but not abandoned, struck down, but not destroyed.

How can we let light shine from our lives if we refuse to forgive? Is your past keeping you from being your best right now? Satan wants us to walk into a big warehouse that is filled with everything that is negative about our lives. He tells us about our failures, and that is all we will ever be; just a failure with a past that can't be healed. But the good news is that Jesus burned that warehouse down. There is healing and restoration in serving Jesus.

FORGIVENESS IS A GIFT TO THE ONE WHO IS HURTING. INNER PEACE CAN ONLY BE REACHED WHEN WE PRACTICE FORGIVING OTHERS AND OURSELVES.

Forgiveness is letting go of the past and letting God control the future. When you can't forgive someone who has deeply wronged you, pray for them. It may not change them but it will always change you.

Forgiveness has absolutely nothing to do with whether or not the person who hurt us deserves to be forgiven. Even after I became a Christian I didn't know how to process all the things that had happened to me. The pain seemed to be even worse as I tried so hard to forgive. I didn't believe God would forgive me unless I was willing to forgive my abusers. I finally realized that forgiveness is not saying that what happened to us was right. It is simply saying we are not responsible for their actions. We must make the decision to forgive; no longer allowing others to hold us in bondage. Giving forgiveness releases in us the power to move forward.

I found myself experiencing emotions I didn't know how to handle. I tried to ignore them, and then I turned to prescription drugs for over twenty years to keep me from feeling the pain. I put my life in fast-forward by setting more goals, and filling my schedule with excessive busyness. Wherever I went or whenever a sermon on forgiveness was preached, I cried for hours because I didn't know how to deal with forgiveness. My life was a mess, I loved the Lord but couldn't talk about the one thing that was holding me back from having that intimate walk I wanted with Jesus. My addiction to prescriptions drugs became stronger and stronger. I did this so I wouldn't have to feel or deal with anything emotionally difficult. In theory, that sounds like it might work, but in real life it causes emotional meltdowns. It also increases physical pain in our bodies, depression, and other illnesses.

As I sit here this morning with tears streaming down my face I realize that in forgiving my abusers I am set free. During the past four years I have watched the life of my friend Alice who had many reasons not to forgive her ex-husband but not only did she forgive but encouraged her children to forgive and have a relationship with their father although he had never done anything for them. Today they sit by their father's side as he is dying. Together they are forgiving him and being bound together with love towards one another. Together they saw their father giving his life to God.

Forgiveness is releasing the pain that was caused by another person and allowing your spirit to fly free. Forgiveness brings peace in the midst of a storm, lifts us up above the transgression of another person's actions and heals our bruised spirit. Today I forgive my father and mother not only with words but from the depths of my heart. In doing so I am being set free. Remember that forgiveness is a gift to the one who is hurting. Forgiving does not mean we deny that the abuse happened. It's refusing to let bitterness rule our lives. Jesus commands us to forgive so that we might be forgiven. We cannot earn God's forgiveness. It is a gift given to each one of us.

I cried out to God to forgive me, then for the next twenty years I tried to earn God's forgiveness. It is not possible to earn God's forgiveness. It doesn't matter how much good you do, you must forgive. God wants us to open our hearts, our clenched fists, and give Him our brokenness. We can't fix it, we can't control it. We simply need to release it unto God. Then He can take all the broken pieces and create a beautiful vessel of honor.

Forgiveness sets us free from being captives to the situation or allowing that situation or person to hold us as prisoners. Forgiveness does not mean we allow that situation or person to abuse or mistreat us again. We are no longer held in Satan's trap when we forgive.

Forgiveness is not pretending the abuse did not happen. It is not denying the shame and pain of all the incidents of physical and sexual abuse, adultery, bulimia, or drug abuse. Forgiveness is learning to run to God, letting go of the situations in your life, and allowing His healing begin to minister to you. When you are too weak to run the race, allow God to carry you.

> Matthew 11:28
> Come to me all who are weary and carry heavy burdens and I
> will give your rest.

Forgiveness is leaving the past behind and not allowing it to control us every hour of every day. I did not know if I could ever forgive myself after experiencing pleasure at times when the abuse happened. The shame, the guilt, the secrets of the abuse were destroying me. But as I begin to realize that not forgiving was destroying my life; I knew it was time to quit pretending the abuse didn't happen. It was time to let go of my need for revenge, control, and accept that what happened didn't destroy me. At one point I rededicated my life to the Lord only to leave the service still unable to forgive my brother.

Do you still carry the heavy burden of resentment, anger, or bitterness because people have hurt or betrayed you? Forgiveness is essential for the healing of our spirit. It's a gift you give to yourself as you forgive those who have sinned against you. Forgiveness is not only a matter of the head; it is a matter of the heart.

Let me give you some reasons why it is hard to forgive.
1. We don't understand how much we have been forgiven.
2. We believe we must forgive instantly.
3. We believe that if we forgive, then we must forget.
4. We believe if we forgive the evil, then the evil will be excused.
5. Many times reconciliation is confused with forgiveness.

God has opened the prison doors of my heart, and then he began to teach me how to walk in forgiveness. He begin to show me that the root of bitterness had taken hold in my life and must be broken in order to forgive. Every chain, every bondage needed to be broken. Our God changes caterpillars into butterflies, sand into pearls, coal into diamonds using time and pressure. He's calling us to break every chain of unforgiveness that has bound us to the past.

The Bible says forgiveness is the willingness to cover the sins of another. It is seeking reconciliation with the offender, and if at all possible restoring a broken relationship. It is cancelling a debt by performing an act of obedience to the Lord. What are some of the reasons you haven't dealt with forgiveness?

To be totally honest, there were layers of pain and issues I had never dealt with. I found that forgiveness was very difficult for me. Carrying around unforgiveness never affected my abusers, I was the one who was putting poison in my body which created all kinds of illness. My parents never did ask for forgiveness, but I finally chose to forgive them. I have found that there is nothing beyond our ability to forgive if we ask God to first forgive us and walk in the truth of His word. Although living a forgiving lifestyle doesn't change the past, it transforms you and changes your future.

The healing may be instantaneous, or it may be a process. Ask for healing and trust God for the restoration. Sometimes we feel God is asleep at the wheel of our lives- we can't sense Him doing anything about our problems but His presence with us is enough. When God says enough is enough, He restores us. Every hard thing we endure can put us in touch with our desire for God. Every trial we go through can strengthen that desire until it becomes a consuming fire within us and a passion to experience God's unconditional love.

Everything is possible with God. No stone is left unturned when we submit to God. He never leaves us; His love and compassions never cease. Unmeasurable love is ours if we seek Him and serve Him.

In the year of 2012, I told God I wanted to completely surrender to Him. I wanted to be like Mary and sit at the feet of Jesus and learn of Him. And then I asked God what He required of me. His reply was total and radical obedience. Back then, I had been obedient in as far as my knowledge of what God required of me; but I wasn't honest with myself. I had faith but I had not really practiced that faith, believing that God could deliver me from my past. I was full of knowledge yet starved to really know how to have an intimate walk with the Lord. My heart cried out to God and He begin to show me my disobedience in my walk with Him. I needed to die to my carnal desires and trust God totally. Radial obedience to God means I am no longer in control-GOD IS!

Beside the physical scars from my past, I also had emotional wounds that needed healing. After pretending my emotional scars didn't exist, and wearing different masks to conceal them from others, it was time to remove the masks one by one. I cried out to God for forgiveness because I needed His forgiveness in order to forgive my abusers. In Him we have redemption through his blood, the forgiveness of sins, in accordance with the riches of God's grace that he lavished on us with all wisdom and understanding. Ephesians 1: 7-8

Dark periods in life come to all of us, times when we feel as if the chains of sin and destruction cannot be broken, that we are in a prison and can never be set free. Let's take a brief look at the apostle Paul and Silas. Paul and Silas were chained to a wall in total darkness with bloody stinging backs. They did not despair, they rejoiced. They prayed and sang hymns to God. All the prison doors opened, and the prisoners' chains came loose. Forgiveness was loosed that night as Paul and Silas praised God. That same jailor believed and he and his family were baptized that very night.

Do your circumstances sometimes feel like a prison cell from which there is no escape? Does darkness surround you and pain overwhelm you? Begin to sing and praise God and see the walls come crumbling down. God has healing for you and me. It is a process, don't give up. He has promised to bind up the brokenhearted and comfort all who mourn.

The choice was mine. Would I walk in it? Could I see His grace and love for me? Would I be able to face the pain, forgive, and walk that intimate holy walk with Him? I didn't think I could because I knew a chamber of my heart was still filled with so much pain that I didn't want to face.

Who am I not to forgive? I want to go past the outer court; yes, walk into the most Holy Place; reside where you, Lord, dwell and fall to my knees and cry out forgive me, for I have sinned against you. I want to reach out and touch you, just the hem of your garment. I want to sit at your feet and worship and then find a place of forgiveness; forgiving and being forgiven; for that is my desire. I am no better than the criminal that was crucified on the cross beside you. Jesus, please remember me when you come into your Kingdom; for I want to be with you cleansed and made holy, yes totally forgiven. I want to walk and talk with you and be cleansed by the blood of the Lamb; with the chains of unforgiveness broken. It is your mercy and grace setting me free. Jesus, I want to hear the words not guilty, no longer condemned.

My question to you today would be do you know the man called Jesus? The man, who with one word wipes the past away. Can you see His great love; as he utters, that one word forgiven, my child, you are forgiven. Do you feel the peace? Peace that only He can give as He says gently unto you, you are forgiven.

Satan wants to weigh us down with guilt, shame, and a mind that does not want to forgive. If he can keep us bound we will never make our way to the cross. We will never be set free, or our bondage broken. Does the trauma of your past paralyze you from moving forward and being set free? Are you willing to let someone help you?

If you are struggling to forgive, just think through the following questions. Am I aware of how much I have been forgiven by God?
1. Am I trying to forgive too quickly or am I dragging my feet?
2. Am I trying to work forgiveness out or am I sweeping it under the rug?
3. Am I afraid that in forgiving I am condoning the evil of sexual abuse or other sins that have been committed against me?
4. Has anyone forgiven you?
5. Will you trust God to help you to forgive?
6. Who benefits from having a forgiving heart?
7. Does forgiveness heal the forgiver more than the one who is forgiven?

"Forgive people in your life, even those who are not sorry for their actions. HOLDING ON TO ANGER ONLY HURTS YOU NOT THEM."   Written By Spirit Science

FORGIVEN

Have you found the man?
Who with one spoken word
Wipes the past away
The slate is clean
As He whispers forgiven

Forgiven
Can you see His greatness?
As His voice proclaims His love
And cleanses you of all your doubts
Speaks to you, you are mine
I have forgiven you

Forgiven
Do you feel the peace?
As He wipes away your tears
With His nail-scarred hands
Declaring you are mine, my child
I have forgiven you

LOOK AT WHAT GOD DID!

GOD'S PLAN OR MINE

What will it be, my plan or God's plan for my life? I am definitely a planner and like to have things planned down to the last period. But God calls us to walk by faith not by sight, right. I had just finished getting my first book published, set up some book signings and thought I knew what God's plan was.

Two months later I begin to set into motion the next part of what I thought God was calling me to do. I thought I knew what I was going to do- seminars with the Mighty Strong Girls, write, and speak on television talk shows promoting my book, and minister to those who had been abused. It seemed to be the right way as doors were opening up to speak in various cities.

But God had other plans for my life, moving to Georgia and sitting before Him, receiving healing for the wounds of my heart. I needed to refocus, sit at the feet of Jesus and meditate and pray.

> Matthew 11:38
> He said come to me, all you who are weary and burdened and I
> will give you rest.

I was much too busy and thought I could stubbornly muddle through all the changes in my own strength. I needed healing of sexual abuse, broken relationships, control issues, and prescription drug addiction; all before I would be equipped to minister to others with the compassion and love of God. Knowledge of the Word, and counseling skills were not enough to equip me to minister as God desired. I needed a closer walk with God.

God opened the doors for me to move to Georgia. It seemed like everything was falling in place although I was troubled about leaving some friends and relationships behind. For over a year I had been asking God for a more intimate relationship with him. But I was too busy with my frantic schedule of writing, speaking, teaching, dating, and working in my church to just sit down and spend quality time with God. I attended every service at my church, was active in various ministries, and prayed with my pastor. I was involved with three other prayer groups still wanting something different from God. It seemed like my relationship with God was all about doing things instead of sitting at His feet and listening.

My life seemed to be nothing but a roller coaster of ups and downs. What was I missing? I begin to fast and pray and ask God to show me his way that I might be more like Him. When we have done something that is displeasing to God- we are miserable until we come and confess it to Him. King David experienced that same feeling. He knew he had done wrong and for days, he avoided dealing with it. He describes his misery and anxiety in these words.

"When I kept silent, my bones wasted away through my groaning all
day long. For day and night your hand was upon me; my strength
was sapped as in the heat of summer." Psalms 32:3-4

I was desperate for a spiritual awakening, healing in my body and spirit. God
moved me out of the main traffic lane to a slower pace. I was weak, torn in wanting
a closer walk with God, but still wanting to hold on to relationships that were det-
rimental to my relationship with God. We, like David who was a man after God's
heart, have to make the same decision David did.

Will we acknowledge our sin, and ask God to forgive us? He tells us, "Then I
acknowledge my sin to you and did not cover up my iniquity." I said, "I will confess my transgression to the Lord and you forgave the guilt of my sin." Psalms 32:5

It was time to let go and let God be in charge. I was miserable, severely
depressed, and I was dragging my feet, reluctantly seeking forgiveness and restoration. God was calling me to higher places, breaking down the dreams I had, and
loving me in the low places. His love is so persistent and steadfast- never ending.
God still had plans for my life, and compassion for me. He never ceased to call me
to come up a little higher and praise Him. His master plan brings victory. When
I was defeated, exhausted, and thought I could not take one more step; still He
declared His love for me and said I have a greater plan, one that you can't see.
Follow me. I will restore unto you all that was taken away, I will heal your shame,
forgive your guilt, take away the darkness in your heart and set you free from the
addiction of prescription drugs.

As I sat before God one day He spoke to me that I wanted to microwave my
recovery, again that problem of trying to be in control and do it my way. But He
said, my child I only want to maximize my time with you and love you through
your pain that you might follow my plan for your life. I love you too much for you
not to gain full recovery. You asked me for an intimate walk. Open yourself fully
to my presence. I love you and will not leave you to struggle alone.

GOD SAID MY PLANS WILL NOT BE THAWARTED.
I HAVE THE LAST WORD. TRUST ME.

The nails in my hands, my pierced side, and the crown of thorns placed upon
my head, all of this I would have done if it was only for you. I want to heal your
deepest wounds, give you peace and freedom to praise me joyfully and completely.

He interrupted my plans with His love. His compassion was overwhelming.
I couldn't fathom this type of love. He sent people into my life that loved me,
prayed for me and hung in there every step of the way as I fought the depression.
They encouraged me to not give up, to take the next step towards freedom and to
praise God for He will bring you through.

I can assure you of one thing, God is bigger than all your problems. He cares even when we continue to ask. "Why God" Why must I go through this trial? Our difficulty is that we have a mind to ask questions, but do we have enough insight to understand the answers. I believe God set life up this way as a test of our faith. Will you trust God with your life?

Ruth Bell Graham, wife of evangelist Billy Graham, put it so beautifully when she wrote the following:

> I lay my "whys?'
> Before your cross
> In worship kneeling,
> My mind beyond all hope,
> My heart beyond all feeling;
> And worshipping,
> Realize that I,
> In knowing you,
> Don't need a "why?"

Why did Jesus die for us? Why did He go to the cross, the sinless Son of God? Simply because of His great love for each one of us.

How can I continue to ask "WHY?" when Jesus paid the ultimate price for my freedom and healing? Even so, I still wanted my recovery to be quick, I just wanted to microwave the process. God spoke to my heart that first day when I wanted to complete the process my way and simply said to me: It may be quick but it may be a process. It's not your choice, it's mine. Trust me fully and praise me when you feel like you can't go any further. I will love you to the end. You will have the victory if you let go and trust me. My love and grace are so amazing.

GOD YOU LOVED ME WHEN I SELFISHLY DEMANDED IT BE DONE MY WAY IN MY TIME. YOU INTERRUPTED MY LIFE WITH YOUR LOVE AND STILL I WANTED IT DONE MY WAY.

God, this path of drug recovery seems so long and it's only been six days. I know you could deliver me instantly but you haven't promised that to me. I sound like the Israelites when they complained about being in the wilderness with no water to drink and only manna to eat. Each time I have prayed about it you have said you want to maximize my time with you so that I could learn to depend on you and trust you through the process. You are a God that keeps your promises so I will wait on you, pray more, and read your word. But this I know, I need you every hour of every day. This is one of the most difficult processes I have worked through, but I know someday I will proclaim that victory is mine. You are my deliverer, all that I need to overcome.

Nine days into recovery from drug abuse. I am so tired, so much to do. I will just sit at your feet, pray and worship you. I will exalt you even as I struggle each day of this process, for you are my King, my Savior, and all things are possible through you.

I am so tired, just want to give up but you've told me to hold on to your unchanging hand, and you will deliver me. One month and five days! I am determined with God's help to succeed. Praise God for one night of nine hours of sleep. So tired. Please give me your sweet sleep tonight.

Lord, I cry out to you today. You are my God. Keep me safe as I walk through this time of trouble. I am weak but you are strong. Have mercy on me. O' God I call unto you. Give me the strength to be an overcomer and I will praise you. Even now Lord, I will praise you in the midst of the storms. You are my only rock, my only peace, my refuge, my portion in the land of the living. I will claim you as my deliverer. Do not hide your face from me Lord. Cause me to see, to know, that you have a perfect plan for my life, that this is just a period of being tested. You have promised from your Word, though I walk through the valley you are with me. You have asked me not to fear, for you have redeemed me. Though I pass through the waters, I will not drown, when I walk through the fire, I will not be burned. You are an all-consuming fire and you will bring me through the fire of suffering to be as gold for your service. You are making a way in the desert and streams in the wasteland of my life.

I will give you praise, honor, glory for you are doing a new work in my life. Without you I will surely fail. I want to have a faith that stands against any obstacle that is placed in my life, a faith that grows and is totally committed to you.

I thought I was going to make it, then I collapsed and ended up in intensive care for eleven days. The doctor didn't think I would come out of the hospital. I had emergency surgery and was very ill. I couldn't remember my friends who visited me but I did know that they were all praying for me. I knew that God had my back as my dear friend Alice instructed the doctor that he was not going to put me back on the full dosage of the Xanax. Praise God. What Satan meant for harm God didn't allow to happen. I left the hospital drug free! How good is our God! It was supposed to take a year for me to get off the drug but it ended up being only five months!

I am so grateful that God has taught me to feel, deal, and heal without the drugs. Emotions are messy, too long I have hidden behind the façade of prescription drugs, control issues, and other addictive behaviors not even realizing the power of joy, peace, love and healing you want to complete in my life. It is time to feel, deal, and heal. Sweet Jesus, let the memories be as scars, completely healed. If they rear up their ugly heads let them be as full grown dandelions that with one puff will be blown away. Heal me from the inside out, sweet Jesus I pray. I want to walk in victory and only use the scars to glorify your name, today, tomorrow and forever.

Think upon these things
1. Are you willing to give up the battle and allow Jesus to walk with you?
2. What is holding you back from being delivered from your abusive past?
3. Do you think that prescription drugs, street drugs, sex, or any kind of additive behavior is the answer to your problems?

FEEL! DEAL! HEAL!

Pain overwhelming, just want to run
Can't run far enough to escape anymore
God is everywhere- anywhere- and always near
Pain running down as tears, clouding my vision
I can't escape anymore, it's time to turn around
To feel, deal, and heal!

Shutting out all relationships, can't love anymore
My heart's breaking, it hurts, and I am so angry
Just want to cry, want to be free, but how, when,
Chains wrap me in self-pity, pride rears its ugly head
Demands to be heard, what will people say?
Can't do it, all tangled up in chains- lies that keep me
From feeling, dealing and healing!

Can't control the addictions- so ugly
One pill, how can it make such a difference?
The storm rages, chains of rejection, guilt, and shame
Keep me in bondage, the winds of doubt increase
Just one more pill and the chains of addiction tighten
It's time to turn around, to feel, deal, and heal.

Fire transforms, it changes, it destroys everything
It rages out of control, you must let it go
It doesn't matter what my mother did, nor my father
It only matters that I need to let it go and forgive
Need to trust enough to be honest each day
With myself, others, and you God, my Lord.
Need to desire above all else to let go of the past
To use my experiences to minister to others
To feel, deal, and heal.

All prisons don't have bars, walls that can be seen

Don't have doors with locks, sometimes it's just you
Just in your mind, bound by the past, or one little pill
Quit pretending that all things are well
Just let it go as living a lie destroys your reality,
Makes you vulnerable, confuses others
Destroys the real you God has made
Let go and let God. Feel, deal, and heal.

Seek the power of God's presence
His joy will flood your soul
Love so deep will break every chain
Set you free to dance and worship
Can you hear the chains being broken?
One by one they must fall by the wayside
Understand God's unfailing love for you

It's the most powerful weapon
Breaks all bondage, sets you free
It's an unceasing love in the purest form
In the midst of the darkest hour, the deepest valley
On the highest mountain, everywhere you go
Never ceases, only seeks our highest good
Sets us free to find the heart of God
And that's God's perfect plan.
Feel, Deal, and Heal!

Today, August 5th, 2014, I declare I have been set free from the drugs. All praises go to my Lord! Victory is mine! My heart is overwhelmed by how much God loves me. I know that with God's help I can stay completely free. For now, I can deal with the issues of sexual abuse without my masks on, and hiding behind closed doors. God doesn't want us bound by any addiction.

When fear raises its ugly head and accuses us that we can't stay free from addictions, drugs, sexual depravity, overeating, or other controlling substances, we must stand firm; facing our accusers and declare our trust in God. Like David we can declare, our defense is of God, who saves the upright in heart.

If you are confronted with a crisis that threatens to destroy you, don't quit, don't give up, and don't run back to believing you can't stay free. Respond with the word's David said, "I will trust in the Lord." David stood up to the problems in his life by placing all of his trust in God. The Bible says, "Trust in the Lord with all your heart, and lean not on your own understanding. In all your ways acknowledge Him and He shall direct your paths. Proverbs 2:5-6

Stand up to life by placing your trust in God and not circumstances. This includes accepting responsibility for your life. Choices have consequences. You are an addict by choice. You are a food junkie or alcoholic by choice. You are an adulterer by choice. You can be delivered from sexual abuse. Quit playing the blame game. You are today what you decided to be yesterday. The world is full of people running from life, hiding behind masks. Don't just take off the masks, destroy them, and embrace life by speaking the truth of the Word into your life daily.

Stand up to life, serving God with all that is within you. Stand up to life by realizing who you are and whose you are. You are a child of the Most High God. You are created in the image of God, and God does not quit. In the Garden of Gethsemane, knowing the agony before Him, Jesus said "not what I will but what you will." Mark 14:30. He went to the cross, and suffered shame. He died with disgrace and thieves, and was buried in a borrowed grave. But He did not quit! He arose from the grave and now sits at the right hand of God. (Hebrew 12:2) Don't quit you'll soon be with Him, too.

One year later, August 20th, 2015 I declare:

I am still standing though fiery trials surround me
My strength is weak, but like Shadrach, Meshach, and Abednego,
I will declare my God is able to deliver me
When I walk through the fire, I shall not be burned
I will still be standing when life all around is changing
Like Daniel, I refuse to bow down to another God
When I am mocked, I will still trust and obey
I will worship my God and I will still be standing.

When my faith is shaken, and my feet stumble
And Satan mocks me saying, where is your God now?
I will declare God has set my feet upon solid ground
And to God alone will I bow and declare my victory.
I will declare you are my God, giving me strength to win
When the floods of uncertainty and fear assail
I have planted my feet on the solid rock
In you God I take shelter, you are my refuge

I am reclaiming the territory that I had abandoned
Broken, I run to you, falling on my knees crying
Offering all of me to the King of Kings
You are all this heart is living for now
Your touch restores my life, sets me free

So I bow before you, surrendering all of me.
Your interruption of love has made me whole
I am purified by fire, made holy and acceptable

I encountered the power of Jesus' blood
Thirsty for living water, I come drinking at the fountain
At the river of His amazing love and forgiveness.
Reclaiming the territory I had abandoned
Placing my broken cracked vessel in the Potter's hand
To be restored perfectly by the Master's hand.
The chains of sin are breaking, one by one
Can't you hear them falling?

There's power in the name of Jesus
Power to break every chain, to set the captive free
Truth and unconditional love for you and me
Deliverance in the name of Jesus
The windows of heaven opened to me
Broke the chains that had me bound
Set me free to praise you, shouting Hallelujah
I will shout it out! I am free!
Praise His name, I have the victory!
My God delivers and sets us free!

MY DECLARATION OF FAITH

I declare the only addiction I shall have is to Jesus, my King and Lord. Now my heart's desire is to be addicted to Jesus- not drugs. Not bound by the sins of my past, and not bound by sexual abuse. God is in the healing business and all my praise goes to Him!

Addicted to Jesus

They tell me everything is going to be all right
Why should I worry what tomorrow will bring
Nothing can trouble me that you don't already know
So I'll stand and claim YOU ARE MY PROTECTOR.
You are the water I can walk on, no way shall I drown
You are the fire I walk thru, no way shall I be burned,
So I'll stand and claim YOU ARE MY WAYMAKER.
I can't move the mountains without you.
It's your presence that gives me LIFE AND FAITH
The strength to believe that all things are possible
Can't pray without you- you are GOD MY FATHER
Can't live without you, you are LIFE ETERNAL

They tell me everything is going to be alright
So I'll stand and claim YOU ARE MY LORD.
Blessings come down as praises go up
Every step I take, I hold to God's unchanging hand
Every breath I take, I breathe in your fragrance
You are IN THE ATMOSPHERE, THE AIR I BREATHE
Need you near, need you to hear my praises
I love you. I love you, my King and Savior.

I love you, I love you. YOU ARE WORTHY OF PRAISE

Jesus, you are the all SUFFICIENT ONE
The one thing I cannot do without
You are my PEACE as the storm rages
I'll rise up and dance before you as David did
Bow before you in adoration, cry out for mercy
Walk before you in holiness, FOR YOU ARE HOLY
JESUS YOU ARE MY VICTORY, MY DELIVERER.

Though the storm continues to rage,
And Satan tries his best to destroy me,
God, you raised me up though death tried to steal me
You placed upon the television screen the words
You cannot die before your appointed time
I didn't bring affliction to destroy you, but to grow you
So take your next step of faith and grow in me
Once again God reached out with His unchanging hand
Calling me to glory in, thru, and above the afflictions
To embrace His will for my life with a fresh anointing.

I am dancing in the rain, through the pain
Praising God, moving into the mighty river
Releasing all burdens. Surrendering all control
Just praising God for His mercy endures forever
Shouting praises, all praises to the King of Kings
What a mighty God I serve!

Therefore, since Christ suffered in His body, arm yourselves also with the same attitude, because he who has suffered in his body is done with sin. As a result, he does not live the rest of his earthly life for human desires, but rather for the will of God. I Peter 4:1-2. Praise God!

The Chains are Broken

Freedom from sin, forgiveness of the past
Chains of abuse broken, destroyed forever
How can it be? Surrender and I was forgiven.
Victory was mine as I bowed before God
The chains of abuse, each link was broken
Guilt, shame, denial, and anger
They kept me bound so tightly, all broken
Sweet peace from on high was given to me

Victory was mine as I bowed before God
Unconditional love was given to me
Forgiven, yes forgiven today
Delivered from all bondage, given liberty
I boldly told Satan to get thee behind
Your power has been broken, shattered forever
Condemnation I will no longer accept
Freedom and victory are mine today

Romans 5:3-5, 15-18
Not only so, but we also rejoice in our sufferings, because we know that suffering produces perseverance, perseverance character; and character, hope. And hope does not disappoint us, because God has poured out His love into our hearts by the Holy Spirit, whom He has given us. How much more did God's grace and the gift that came by the grace of the one man, Jesus Christ, overflow to the many! Again, the gift of God is not like the result of one man's sin: The judgment followed one sin and brought condemnation, but the gift followed many trespasses and brought justification. For if by the trespass of one man, death reigned through that one man, how much more will those who receive God's abundant provision of grace and the gift of righteous reign in life through the one man, Jesus Christ.

SHOUT IT OUT!
GOD'S LOVE INTERRUPTS OUR LIVES!
GOD'S LOVE DELIVERS AND SETS FREE!

Jesus You Have Captured My Heart!

I embrace my femininity
The woman that God made
Beauty that God has restored
Yes, I embrace intimacy
With my creator, my bridegroom
Peace and joy flood my heart
Because I am loved, I am His own
He calls me His Beloved
His bride to be.

Through the flood and the flame
Through the fire of brokenness
He has never forsaken me
Though the waters overtake me
I shall not drown
Though the fire be all about me,
I shall not be burned
For I have come to sit at His feet
Jesus, the consuming fire.

My Protector, His presence is so near
As He passionately pursues my heart
I am so secure in His love walking with Him.
For He has been good to me
He gave me His shield of victory
His hand ever sustains me
Close by His side I will remain
His mercies are new every morning
His love sustains and upholds me
I need never to walk in fear again

He protects from trouble
Surrounds me every hour
With beautiful songs of deliverance.
His sacrifices are a broken spirit
A broken and contrite heart
Sacrifices that never cause pain
He does not demand, betrayal is not His way
Only unfailing love for you and me
To sustain and restore us to greater praise

What a mighty God we serve. Bow before Him, adore Him and arise to serve Him. He is worthy of all praise! GOD, the Master Potter delights in changing lives and setting us free to worship Him. Nothing on earth can keep us bound if we surrender to Him. He takes the disgrace we experienced and turns it into victory. He takes the unrest and fear we have endured and turns it into overflowing peace and joy. God extends grace and healing to each one of us who have walked in darkness and brokenness. You can experience His unconditional love and rejoice as He heals the broken places in your life. The woman you will then see in the mirror will be a reflection of the Christ in her. Psalms 34:5 "They looked to Him and were radiant, and their faces were not ashamed."

Linda is the author of Broken Chains written in 2013. She has had poems published in Across the Way, Whispers in the Wind, Mighty Strong Girls and various other magazines. She was the winner of the World of Poetry Golden Poet Award in 1987.

Linda's desire is to minister to and encourage women and children to overcome life-hindering problems. She was actively involved in bereavement ministry for over ten years. She developed a Christian based bereavement ministry, writing her own curriculum and taught seminars for over ten years.

Linda resides in Buford, Georgia. She attends Friendship Baptist Church of Duluth, Georgia. She can be reached through her e-mail address of lkbrapture@G.mail

CPSIA information can be obtained
at www.ICGtesting.com
Printed in the USA
LVOW01s2030120416

483323LV00001B/1/P

9 781498 468084